"*Reimagining Education* is a landmark contribution to the education debate. Drawing on the painstaking analysis of contributions from thousands of children and young people, the authors place their voices – so often overlooked – front and centre. Despite the range and richness of these testimonies, a strikingly consistent message emerges: huge numbers of children and young people are suffering because of the way in which the education system is currently configured. In this context, maintaining the status quo is not just unsustainable – it is indefensible. What makes this book so powerful is that it doesn't stop at critique. Drawing on the principles of self-determination theory – autonomy, competence and relatedness – it offers a compelling vision of what a more humane, inclusive, psychologically-informed education system would look like. If you want to know what young people really think about school – and what they need instead – look no further."

James Mannion, Director of *Rethinking Education*

"This gem of a book is an extraordinary triumph: proof that not only is it possible to capture and raise up the voices of children and young people, but also imperative; necessary. Here we find children's direct words and experiences woven seamlessly into psychological theory, tracking into implications for practice which will undoubtedly stir and inspire the thoughts and hearts of its readers. To echo a metaphor threaded through this seminal work, the sea change called for here is on the horizon. Will the education system, and every cog and person within it, answer the call?"

Dr Nicole Schnackenberg, Child, Community and Educational Psychologist

"A powerful and thought-provoking read that invites us all to truly 'Think Differently'. This book brilliantly captures the heart of relational practice, offering both inspiration and theory-based guidance. Through insightful reflections and actionable models, it lays out a compelling vision for creating psychologically and physically safe schools where every individual feels a genuine sense of belonging. A must-read for anyone committed to transforming education through connection and care."

Phil Willott, Director of Education, Raleigh Education Trust

"*Reimagining Education* offers a rare invitation to see school life through the eyes of children, focusing on the rules and relationships that shape their daily experiences. Too often, education is viewed only through the lens of adults who choose to be there, while the voices of students are overlooked. This book redresses that balance, thoughtfully considering the impact of schooling on well-being from both perspectives. A must-read for anyone seeking to deepen their understanding of the systems that shape children's lives."

Sarah Johnson, Author, Director of Phoenix Education Consultancy and PRUsAP President

Reimagining Education

"School is too much pressure." Drawing from relational and trauma-informed approaches, *Reimagining Education* explores ways to design and sustain a successful school system, through the eyes and experiences of children and young people.

Chapters consider a range of themes, from mentally healthy schools to attendance and academic pressure, to build the vision of a compassionate school where no child is left behind or excluded. Each topic is introduced through the voices and views of children, who reflect on their experiences and tell us what would make it better and create a sense of belonging for all. These themes are explored alongside key psychological theory, before accessible strategies and recommendations for change are introduced.

Centring the views of children and young people, this essential guide focuses on developing an education system fit for the workforce of the future, based on skills, humanity, compassion, and citizenship. It will be valuable reading for all teachers, pastoral staff, educational leaders, and educational psychologists.

Maddi Popoola is a service manager for the Mental Health Support Team in Nottingham City. She has been working in various roles within education since 2004, including mainstream primary, secondary, and alternative provision settings. Maddi qualified as an Educational Psychologist (EP) in 2018 and is the co-founder of a mental health support website, www.NottAlone.org.uk.

Sarah Sivers has worked as a Child, Community and Educational Psychologist for over 11 years and with children and young people with additional needs for over 20 years. She has engaged in pupil views research to explore children and young people's views and experiences and to use what they have shared to generate discussions and create change.

Louise McDonagh has worked in a range of schools since 2006, including in a role as Vice Principal in an inner-city academy, with responsibility for safeguarding and behaviour. Louise has also been a member of a Mental Health Support Team, leading on whole school approaches to mental health and trauma-informed approaches.

Reimagining Education

Hearing Children's Voices to Design Schools Where All Belong

Maddi Popoola, Sarah Sivers, and Louise McDonagh

Routledge
Taylor & Francis Group
LONDON AND NEW YORK

Cover image: Juliet Hardy (aged 10)

First published 2026
by Routledge
4 Park Square, Milton Park, Abingdon, Oxon OX14 4RN

and by Routledge
605 Third Avenue, New York, NY 10158

Routledge is an imprint of the Taylor & Francis Group, an informa business

© 2026 Maddi Popoola, Sarah Sivers, and Louise McDonagh

The right of Maddi Popoola, Sarah Sivers, and Louise McDonagh to be identified as authors of this work has been asserted in accordance with sections 77 and 78 of the Copyright, Designs and Patents Act 1988.

All rights reserved. No part of this book may be reprinted or reproduced or utilised in any form or by any electronic, mechanical, or other means, now known or hereafter invented, including photocopying and recording, or in any information storage or retrieval system, without permission in writing from the publishers.

Trademark notice: Product or corporate names may be trademarks or registered trademarks, and are used only for identification and explanation without intent to infringe.

British Library Cataloguing-in-Publication Data
A catalogue record for this book is available from the British Library

ISBN: 978-1-032-98080-5 (hbk)
ISBN: 978-1-032-98063-8 (pbk)
ISBN: 978-1-003-59693-6 (ebk)

DOI: 10.4324/9781003596936

Typeset in Optima
by Apex CoVantage, LLC

Contents

Prologue ix

Introduction 1

1 Staff wellbeing and mental health: Putting on your oxygen masks first 13
Louise McDonagh

2 Fear and rules: The views of children on the state of the current system 27
Louise McDonagh

3 Relationships, relationships, relationships 45
Sarah Sivers

4 What will it take to create a genuine meaning of the term "mentally healthy schools"? 67
Maddi Popoola

5 Academic pressure through the eyes of children: What do they really want to learn? 90
Maddi Popoola

6 What do children out of school say about their experiences in mainstream education? 109
Maddi Popoola

7 Attendance, the LA, and the wider system 130
Jennifer Hardy

Contents

8 **The Covid legacy: What has been lost, missed, and gained?** **138**
Sarah Sivers

9 **What can we do better? From the views of children and school staff** **156**
Maddi Popoola, Louise McDonagh, and Sarah Sivers

Index 170

Prologue

It's not easy to sit with that noun, as it's not something any of us thought we would do in our careers. We have all worked with children, teachers, teaching-assistants and the vast array of other staff members who keep the cogs of schools turning, day in day out. Between the three of us, we bring over 60 years of experience within the education system to the table. None of us can imagine doing anything that doesn't involve the welfare and education, in some way, of children and young people. Yet, across those 60-plus years, we feel an increasing frustration, sometimes anger, sometimes hopelessness, when we consider the education system we are working within. We have seen various governments tinker around the edges: coursework turned into controlled assessments, turned into terminal exams; knowledge-based curriculums; skills, skills, skills; the increased use of and normalisation of managed moves; the tsunami of permanent exclusions; the rise of alternative provisions (including the rising costs of such provisions), against the backdrop of a growing mental health crisis in our children. So much has changed, and yet, at the core, so much has stayed exactly the same. A colleague of ours, who spent years in mainstream education as a head teacher, described it clearly but bleakly:

> Education works for about 80 to 85% of children. You have really clear rules and systems, which can work for those children . . . but what about the other 15–20% that want to be at school, but just can't? We've tried to bring a business model into a system, plus a recruitment and retention crisis. We haven't got a system to pick up those kids.

We know that those children are the thin edge of the wedge, and the reality is that whilst the 80–85% are *coping*, **are they happy?** Are they in a system which makes them feel safe and included? Does their education make them feel excited to learn? Is what we are teaching them important?

Prologue

Increasingly, and especially post-pandemic, all three of us feel that we are reaching a crisis point in our education system. More and more children, and their families, are opting out (not always through choice) from a system that is creating more harm than good for them. Those still working through the system don't always fare much better. Acknowledging this and struggling with it are what led us to write this book. We knew we needed to be frank and honest about what the issues are, but we also wanted to offer alternatives to what is currently being done.

Who are we?

Dr Maddi Popoola

I have been working in various roles within education since 2004, including mainstream primary, secondary, and alternative provision settings in Nottingham, London, and internationally (Shanghai, China). This has given me extensive experience of working as part of and leading pastoral teams in education settings, developing an in-depth understanding of school systems, processes, and working with a diverse range of professionals and students. This has included working closely with senior leadership teams and in a multi-agency capacity with the wider professional networks around a school. I have led on projects within education to support and embed whole school mental health and wellbeing, including delivering training and supporting staff and students on an individual and group basis. I have also had extensive experience of working with children and young people in a therapeutic way, using a range of therapeutic and evidence-based approaches such as EMDR, CBT, and Narrative Therapy.

I qualified as an Educational Psychologist (EP) in 2018, I worked in Derby City and Nottingham City after graduating the Doctoral Programme, and as well as carrying out the vast range of duties typical to the role of an EP I have been involved in local and national projects, such as the "pupil views" research, national piloting of the ATTEND programme for non-attenders and the Wellbeing Return to Education project. I am proud to be the co-founder of a local mental health support website (www.NottAlone.org.uk), which provides users with resources and referral pathways for help and support from both local and national mental health support services. The NottAlone podcast is a new venture that is a way of getting the conversations that need to be had about mental health support out there, particularly to our local community. I am currently very proud to be leading a large team of amazing individuals, working as a service manager for the Mental Health Support Team (MHST) in Nottingham City.

Dr Sarah Sivers

I have worked as a Child, Community, and Educational Psychologist for over 11 years, and I have worked with children and young people with additional needs for over 20 years. I work therapeutically using Acceptance and Commitment Therapy, trauma-informed approaches, and Solution-Focused Psychology to inform my work. I believe in life-long learning, which is why I continue to develop new skills, such as training as a Play Therapist.

Learning new skills has meaning for me and it enables me to provide much-needed wellbeing support to children and young people. It is vital to me to include and involve the children and young people I work with, to do with rather than do to. This is why I have engaged in pupil views research to explore children and young people's views and experiences and to use what they have shared to generate discussions and create change.

I am also involved with other projects, which focus on developing and sharing psychologically informed thinking around education and wellbeing. This includes a webinar series, called EP Reach-Out, that my wonderful colleague Dr Nicole Schnackenberg and I created in April 2020. EP Reach-Out is a platform for sharing innovative work that supports children, young people, and everyone who cares for and supports them. It brings together research, projects, and thinking from across psychology and education and is a joy to be part of.

I am excited to continue this psychologically informed work and generate new ways of thinking about and delivering education that is motivating, meaningful, and enjoyable (for children, young people, and the adults supporting them).

Louise McDonagh

I qualified as a teacher in 2006 but had known since I was about 6 years old that I wanted to work in a school. Since I first started teaching English in a secondary school in Nottingham, I knew my passion lay in the pastoral care

Prologue

of young people. My career followed a trajectory towards eventually becoming Vice Principal in an inner-city academy, with responsibility for safeguarding and behaviour. This was a baptism of fire and was one of the reasons I am able to understand and empathise with the array of challenges facing school staff today. It was only later in my career that I started to explore Psychology, earning a Master's in the discipline. It was then that I really began to question the practices and philosophies of the schools I had worked in and with. I later worked for a Mental Health Support Team (MHST), leading on whole school approaches to mental health and trauma-informed approaches. I also have experience of working in the international sector, within the British system; seeing how the system tries to squeeze square pegs into round holes, even with students from wealthier backgrounds.

Education should set us free, but currently it feels like a yoke for too many of our young people; let's change that.

How this book works

While this book is a collaboration between the three authors, we each have our own style, our own personal experiences within the education system, and our own passions and interests. Therefore, you will hear three unique voices throughout the book, but with two golden threads running throughout: the need to listen to what children are saying to us and the urgent need to approach things differently. The following summary provides a brief overview of each chapter in this book.

Introduction	"Every child has the right to express their views, feelings and wishes in all matters affecting them, and to have their views considered and taken seriously." – Article 12: United Nations Convention on the Rights of the Child, 1989 We have written the Introduction together to explore the necessity for this book and give you a flavour of what will be discussed throughout the chapters.

Chapter 1 **Staff wellbeing and mental health:** Putting on your oxygen masks first	"I'm a person who likes to be as organised . . . proactive as possible . . . The first half term . . . has taken all of that away from me. I felt quite exposed. Quite vulnerable." – School DSL and Year Leader This chapter was written by Louise and feels personal to her, having worked in environments that have nurtured and supported staff, but also in those that have created fear and anxiety. She suggests ways to improve staff wellbeing, which in turn creates a system that supports children, too.
Chapter 2 **Fear and rules:** The views of children on the state of the current system	"School rules are strict. I lose time learning which is supposed to be the most important thing, for something stupid like talking in line." – Child Louise has written this chapter, drawing on her two decades of experience as a teacher and leader in a range of schools and in a range of roles. This chapter examines what is driving the behaviour systems that are used so frequently across schools, with little reflection, and what could work more effectively.
Chapter 3 **Relationships, relationships, relationships**	"Going to school and connecting with my friends really helps me and i enjoy it but i do think we don't get enough time to do so at all." – Young person This chapter, written by Sarah, draws on her experiences of working therapeutically with children and explores how the education system needs to embrace trauma-informed approaches to relationships in schools.
Chapter 4 **What will it take to create a genuine meaning of the term "mentally healthy schools"?**	"Mental health needs to be as important as grades." – Child Maddi uses her knowledge and experiences both as an EP and MHST manager to unpick what is happening in the education system from a mental health perspective. What steps are being taken in the right direction, but what roadblocks do we still need to overcome?

Prologue

Chapter 5 **Academic pressure through the eyes of children: What do they really want to learn?**	*"I don't like exams and find it hard to show all I know in them. I'm dyslexic and it doesn't enable me to show my strengths."* – Child *"I feel like my grades define me as a person."* – Child In this chapter Maddi gets to grips with one the most controversial topics within our current system: the curriculum and exams. With external testing from age 6 to 18, how can we assess what has been learnt more humanely, and how can we ensure that what children are learning is valuable and valued?
Chapter 6 **What do children out of school say about their experiences of mainstream education?** We're in an attendance crisis, but what do children out of school say about their experiences in mainstream education? Why would a child not want to attend school?	*"Sometimes I just felt overwhelmed by the amount of work and all the people at school. I just need time alone to get a break from it all. After a while I felt really low and couldn't get motivated for anything."* – Child This chapter was written by Maddi and asks children directly: Why do you not want to go to school? Using their feedback and insights, she unpicks the key obstacles to attendance and what we can do about them.
Chapter 7 **Attendance, the LA, and the wider system**	This chapter is an insert provided for us by Jennifer Hardy, a local authority (LA) head of service for access to learning. Jen describes some of the key pressures felt by LAs and the role and responsibilities of the LA, particularly linked to exclusion and attendance.
Chapter 8 **The Covid legacy: What has been lost, missed, and gained?**	*"I am worried about catching up with my school work."* – Child Sarah explores the ongoing impact of Covid-19 on children in this chapter. Using children's voices from her research, she questions what lessons could be learned from the time spent in lockdown as well as the "new normal" that came afterwards, and wonders how we successfully move on from this momentous event.

Chapter 9 **What can we do better? From the views of children and school staff**	*"I think that the school should educate us about being positive, building up self-esteem and body positivity."* – Child "Education must develop every child's personality, talents and abilities to the full." – Article 29: United Nations Convention on the Rights of the Child, 1989 In our conclusions and recommendations for policy makers, together we look at the bigger picture. What do we need to do to create a system that serves all? We draw all of these ideas and suggestions together, and also suggest other areas that need further consideration.

Introduction

Education and school

The journey of education for any human does not start and end with school, further education, college, or even university. We can try to look through a narrow lens and define learning through the structured opportunities school presents to children. When we think of school the images that come to mind in relation to learning have been constructed by a culture of school being classroom-based, often with a teacher at the front of the class giving instruction and knowledge, with children sitting in rows on plastic chairs listening attentively. Well, those who are "engaged in learning" would be anyway. I am not sure when learning became defined by such expectations and why, but it seems clear, when we think about learning through the wider lens and apply common sense, that learning is a life-long experience, and what we may have "learned" ourselves in the conventional classroom is a fraction of our personal learning journey.

Our hunter–gatherer ancestors are surely the foundation of our understanding of learning. Before the classroom, our children learned for purpose, primarily for survival. A child born into a family would learn through looking and watching, motivated by need and want, an innate desire to be able to "do what you do", because if I learn to make that tool with that stone, I will be able to use it to cut that fruit and eat the juicy part in the middle. Think of the baby, born alone and naked to the world, and the innate need to learn in order for its needs to be met, to grow and thrive, prioritising the need to feel safe and loved, right from the beginning to connect to the caregiver through the basic social interactions of touch, eye contact, physical closeness, and, eventually, mirroring of facial expressions. Following this, learning to crawl, walk, and communicate are all based on desire and need of the things that will benefit human survival and meet innate human needs. I will never forget the frustration in both of my children in the weeks leading up to their first steps, so desperate to reach something on the other side of the room, to walk towards me holding out my arms, driven by such desires to gain the independence and freedom that walking brings, and, of course, to "do what the other humans can do".

Early years education is then a time and chance for learning to continue with the autonomy of self-direction, the endless freedom to choose and learn through play, to watch others and be the master of our learning experiences, to move around freely. As a child reaches school age in the UK, the freedom systematically declines as we move into what has been socially constructed as "learning". Children find themselves seated, through endless periods of listening, inputting information that has been constructed as being pertinent to learn by a system of schooling that sets to define and separate children based on their ability to learn within a set of narrow expectations. In our roles in school we have often observed children in the classroom, usually because they have been identified as having "additional special educational needs", but one has to wonder, with the rise in such needs being so great, is there an argument that the system is creating the "SEND crisis", a term that is now regularly bandied about the UK media.

A pertinent and continually relevant quote often attributed to Aristotle is one that, in school at least, seems to have been forgotten: "education of the mind without education of the heart is no education at all". If we ask ourselves, "what do we want our children to have learned by the time they leave school?", what comes to mind? In *our* experience it is rarely linked to the esteemed academic outcomes upon which so much importance is placed in the mind of the child in the school system. "How to be kind" is one common answer, along with "how to accept others and be tolerant", "to learn what they enjoy and what fulfils, what gives a sense of purpose", "how to be a good friend", and "how to contribute positively to the world". You may have others, based on your own constructs of what is important, but when *we* ask audiences to answer the same question, matters of the heart repeatedly take precedence. Yet, are these the things we place at the centre of the school experience?

Having worked "on the ground" in several schools in the UK, experience of the current system and its flaws have compelled me and my co-authors into a place of advocacy for change. As adults working in the system, it is our responsibility to question the fundamentals and pedagogy that underpin how "school" is being experienced by its "users". We feel a responsibility to ask questions such as "How do children feel about their education?", "What is important to them?", and "How are they impacted upon by their journey through school?"

Through a series of chapters based on themes that have been central to our "pupil views" work over the past five years, this book places a magnifying glass on current practices within education in the UK. In doing so, we believe we have to become uncomfortable with and question ourselves and our belief systems, own our mistakes, and look forward to how we can recreate a school experience that is fit for purpose and ensures all children are prepared to navigate this new world, a world defined by unimaginable advances in technology, and one where an individualist society is increasingly becoming the norm within western culture. The need for change is evident, demonstrated by the new government's curriculum review being already underway. This book will go beyond the idea of schools and imagine education settings as being the cornerstone of a community in which everyone is welcomed.

We hope school leaders, staff, parents, and those connected to the education system will gain ideas from this book, to create a better offering for children of the 21st century. In our most recent pupil views research (Popoola & Sivers, 2023), children attributed school as being the biggest contributing factor to poor mental health, with recurring themes including feelings of pressure and stress, having a lack of autonomy, low sense of competence, and poor relationships.

Our pupil views journey

This book might be written by three authors, but it is informed by so many other voices and collaborations. The most important voices we have been guided, surprised, and humbled by are those of the thousands of children and young people who have shared their views in the research we have conducted over the past five years.

The 23rd of March 2020 is a date that will be remembered by many in the UK as the day lockdown started. This phenomenon we now know as the Covid-19 pandemic was causing uncertainty, fear, and then a change in day-to-day life, the impact of which is still being felt. For those of us working in education, so much changed; schools did remain open, teaching staff worked things out as they went along and did the best they could for vulnerable children and young people and those whose parents were key workers. So much commitment in such difficult circumstances.

Introduction

The way the media reported changes in school life was very different. Just a few weeks into the pandemic reports were claiming that the impact would be devastating with children "missing out". As psychologists and educationalists, we knew there would be an impact, but we didn't have a crystal ball; we didn't know what it would look like, and whatever did happen would not be the result of Covid-19 alone, as there were already deep cracks in the education system.

There was another missing factor, too; these articles were giving an adult viewpoint. Where were the voices, thoughts, and experiences of the children and young people? This is when one of the three authors of this book – Sarah Sivers – decided to create a short online questionnaire to send out to schools in the local authority she worked in (Southend-on-Sea). The aim was to ask children and young people about what was happening for them, whether they were in school or learning at home, and what it was like. When the questionnaire was sent out in May 2020, we did not expect a high number of responses. To be honest it was a project that gave some purpose and focus in what was a confused and uncertain time. A small group agreed to be part of the project, colleagues who at the time were trainee Education Psychologists (EP) (Sarah and Lauren) and an assistant EP (Kate).

Within a few days of the questionnaire being sent to schools we had a couple of hundred responses, and by the time we closed the questionnaire (after ten days) we had 752 responses from children and young people living in the Southend area. We were astounded and then incredibly moved as we began to analyse the data and hear the stories of their experiences. From this data we created a report and presented a webinar to share "What You Told Us" back to the children and young people.

Over a short few weeks this webinar was seen by hundreds of people (predominantly EPs). This included Maddi Popoola and Elaine Looney from Nottingham City Educational Psychology Service. They wanted to replicate the questionnaire in their local area, which they did, and this resulted in a combined report that shared the voices and views of 1,758 children and young people. This work gathered momentum, and we went on to be part of a Pupil Views Collaborative Group with EPs and educational professionals from around the UK.

The Pupil Views Collaborative Group conducted a follow-up survey between October 2020 and March 2021 to explore what the return(s) to school had been like for children and young people. The aim was to again bring the voices of children and young people to the forefront, to hear what they thought and to use their views and experiences to inform our thinking. There were 6,172 children and young people who responded to this survey, giving us insights into their experiences, which we analysed and used to develop suggestions for changes in education.

This work has now been shared in blogs, journal articles, and book chapters; we have presented at a range of conferences, and been interviewed for podcasts and radio shows. We were also invited to provide expert witness evidence for the National Institute for Health and Care Excellence (NICE) panel who were updating the guidelines for Social, Emotional, and Mental Health in Primary and Secondary Schools (NICE, 2022). A fourth follow-up survey was also conducted in 2022–2023 to explore children and young people's views on mental health in more depth, which has also provided us with rich and moving data to understand their experiences.

All of these stories, views, and experiences are at the very centre of this book; our work is informed by all the children and young people who responded to our surveys, plus the children and young people who we continue to work with and listen to. This book also includes the thoughts shared by the teaching staff, professionals, parents, and carers we speak to, plus the colleagues we work alongside. It has been a privilege to gain, hear, and share these experiences; a responsibility we do not hold lightly, and one we will continue to honour.

Core values: Inclusion, humanity, and evidence-based psychology

Inclusion

Our core values and beliefs underpin this book; firstly, that inclusion for all is achievable in schools and that exclusion of children is not a necessity, as it is often proposed by professionals at all levels of the system, from government departments down to members of the school community. A well-known African proverb provides a rich picture of the idea of inclusion, linked to the concept of belonging: "The child who is not embraced by the village will burn it down to feel its warmth". What this refers to, of course, is that a child needs love, connection, and community, and when such needs are not met, the child's cry for help may translate into destructive behaviour, which further exacerbates rejection from the community, and the cycle continues to escalate until, eventually, the child is abandoned completely. We will look more into the behavioural systems in modern schooling and make a case for change. For now, let's consider this concept of "inclusion".

What does inclusion mean?

There are far too many marginalised children in the current system, and behaviour should not be a reason to fail school. The inclusion of children with additional needs has become an increasingly difficult landscape, with mainstream schools finding themselves with a greater amount of need and less resources with which to support these children. However, the foundations of inclusion can be laid without additional resources, and it can be difficult to conceptualise what this "looks" like, often because it is a sense and a feeling. As an "outsider", an Educational Psychologist, who experiences a variety of school environments, this "feeling" is something that is hard to describe. But, in line with the thread of this book being centred on the views of children, what would meaningful inclusion feel like for the child in school?

- Feeling welcome and a sense of belonging; a second home
- Feeling important and valued
- Having meaningful connections with peers and with adults.
- Feeling unique
- Feeling competent
- Feeling supported to participate fully in school without barriers
- Feeling like I can be myself
- Feeling safe
- Experiencing kindness and acceptance

When we think about inclusion, ideas about including those with additional needs may be what comes immediately to mind. For example, how do we meaningfully include the neurodiverse child, or the child with learning needs who struggles to process information, leading to the widening gap in their learning and concerns of this gap becoming even wider, often leading to schools applying for education, health, and care needs assessments (EHCNA) in a bid to be able to provide what they need, or seek an alternative specialist setting. Local authority resources for such settings and the EHCNA applications and assessment process are overwhelmed, with many children ending up out of school because their needs are unable to be met with the current resourcing in mainstream settings. A plethora of reasons may be underpinning the increase in requests for EHC plans, including, in no particular order:

- The impact of the pandemic on child development
- A continued lack of resourcing for mainstream schools
- Additional societal pressures that increase childhood adverse experiences
- Advances in medical care that mean babies can live when born at just 22 weeks gestation

So, when we think about inclusion, we need to think about the current appropriateness and resourcing that is given to the mainstream offer. This includes how specialist services from health, social care, and youth and community groups can be embedded and available in the school community. When you really dig deep into what inclusion means, isn't it absolute madness that because a child doesn't learn in the same way as we expect or doesn't develop in the same way we expect, they should be sent to a specialist institution away from the "normal" kids? What message are we giving to our children about difference and acceptance?

Humanity and connection, difference and acceptance

You may have by now read the tone here, the advocacy for change that is needed to ensure that truly "no child is left behind". To those of us close to the current system, the need for such changes is evident daily, particularly to school staff who work tirelessly to stretch resources as far as they will go.

We need to be clear on the need for inclusion and what message "exclusion" gives to our school community; one of "you're not welcome here", "you don't fit in here". We need to consider the damage that these messages can cause to a human being, as well as what this says about our positioning on humanity, and what it means to be human. Critics would indeed argue that through exclusion we teach lessons of social rules, what is acceptable behaviour if you want to be part of our social community. This is problematic, firstly because in order to create social order and buy-in, a community and its rules must be created and shared by its members, not given by the organisation that sees itself as the ruler; secondly, because we do not meaningfully "teach" or change behaviour through a lack of acceptance of a person's needs or behaviours. In fact, the opposite is true: the more a human feels part of the group and accepted, the more likely they are to conform to the social rules of the group.

This innate human need for socialisation also dates back to our hunter–gatherer ancestors, and our need for survival. Humans did not evolve and survive the test of time purely due to them having more grey matter and consciousness. While this forms part of the picture, much of human success and survival was based on our ability to collaborate and coordinate as part of groups with other humans. This innate desire to belong as part of a group is linked to basic survival instincts – we cannot successfully hunt alone!

Belonging is a key concept that will be addressed throughout this book, so it is important that we understand what it means. Interestingly, belonging is quite the opposite of "fitting in". Fitting in is what people do to feel part of a social group, thereby changing their behaviour or core beliefs in order to be part of the group, and hence survive. To truly belong is to be accepted, just as you are, no matter how much you may get it wrong, or not do, or be the same as other group members. Belonging is therefore a challenging concept to cultivate, because it requires the group to be accepting and inclusive, with an underpinning ethos of understanding of individual differences. This is not to say that the group member who breaks the social rules is accepted for such behaviours, but it does mean that the group will not expel anyone for not fitting in; instead, it means accountability is based on building deep human connections, self-awareness, and empathy. Moreover, if we underpin our social rules with reason, allowing group members to buy in to their importance, rules are much more likely to be followed because the human will accept the rules in order to sustain the successful operation of the group.

Psychology and education

Psychology is everywhere and in everything we do, because we are human. Psychology underpins our understanding of self and others, and psychological theory is being used increasingly across industries to improve team functioning and employee wellbeing, and in incredible ways within the experience of users alongside technology to understand how humans interact with the digital world. An ongoing frustration as a psychologist working within the world of education is the use of outdated (primarily behavioural) psychological theory to inform policy. If you are a parent of a child in the secondary school system in the UK, you will be familiar with the receipt of regular, by the hour, "red or green" updates that are supposed to control and manage behaviour. The red "threat" system supposedly creates a consistent message to children: "Do one thing wrong and this will happen, two things and this will happen", and so on. The difficulty with this, of course, is the subjectiveness of the individual on what constitutes "wrong", and the interaction of this in turn with the child and their sense of the seriousness of the wrongdoing. There seems to be an obsession with reductionist and behavioural methods for managing behaviour, and therein lies the problem, because human behaviour and interaction is impossible to reduce to good and bad. Such concepts are surely in the eye of the beholder, their own belief systems, their own upbringing, their level of patience, and their responses, both verbally and otherwise, that may evoke a response in a child. When I (Maddi) am in a school, delivering training or speaking with school staff in consultation, often-asked questions and comments are "when a child is kicking off, what do I do?" or "They don't care about getting a 'negative point' and disciplining them in this way will often make things worse". My response is usually the same, that there unfortunately cannot be a universal and consistent way of managing these moments because children are individuals, and the need to control such behaviours is born out of adult anxiety. My response is always about one key message: what is your relationship with this child, what do you know about them, what is the purpose of their behaviour, and what are their needs? You may look back to your own education and think about subjects or lessons in which you did better than others. I can almost guarantee that such enjoyment and success is linked to your relationship with the teacher of the lesson, how you perceived their feelings towards you, how they spoke to you when you were out of line, and how this made you feel. The narrative we are given about ourselves from adults rings true to us throughout our lives; despite what we may go on to do or achieve, those voices will remain a part of who we are.

Throughout this book we will use some key psychological theories that we truly believe need to become the underpinning pedagogy for a new school system.

Current systems in schools; what's the problem?

Even the staunchest defender of the current education system that prevails in the UK would have to admit the last ten years have seen a return to more punitive systems of behaviour, a keener focus on rote learning, and a move away from restorative and trauma-informed practices. In fact, therapeutic approaches have been increasingly spoken about with derision by some of the most influential voices in the sector. The slogan "zero tolerance" has largely been dropped, but a cursory review of any number of school behaviour policies, particularly in secondary schools, reveals escalating consequences (usually a euphemism for punishment), stringent control of what children can and can't do, which extends to walking in silence in corridors, and very little meaningful intervention to support students to meet these expectations. Every September a flurry of news stories appear with an unhappy parent frustrated that their child has been punished for wearing patent shoes instead of plain leather, or shoes with Velcro instead of laces. "Shocker: School has rules; more on this as we get it . . ." is frequently the mocking response from proponents of more punitive approaches, who are often the same voices insisting that suspensions are always used as a "last resort".

In 2022/2023 there was a 36% increase in suspensions in the UK compared to the previous year, with children from mixed white and Black Caribbean backgrounds 85% more likely to be suspended. Of course, there are myriad reasons for this increase, including the impact of lockdowns, but are these strict measures having the desired impact? Current attendance data would suggest not; with a recent figure of 39,200 children missing from education (Department for Education, 2024), it would appear that as well as higher numbers of children being prevented from continuing their education, temporarily, an increasing number of children are also opting out and choosing to stay away from a place that should be safe space from the outside world.

The impact of new research through neuroscience on our knowledge of child development and the impact of trauma

Anyone who completed teacher training within the last 15–20 years may have hazy memories of spending an afternoon discussing Piaget and Vygotsky. They may, if they are lucky, have spent an afternoon seminar discussing behaviour, and they may have been told a similar tale to me when I was studying my postgraduate certificate in education (PGCE), that you will "learn how to manage behaviour on the job". In more recent years, trainees and graduates may even have been shown fMRI scans of children's brains, specifically those who have experienced neglect and those from more stable situations. However, in the tumult of many mainstream schools, this consideration of child development, the impact of trauma and Adverse Childhood Experiences (ACEs), and basic child psychology, is soon forgotten.

Introduction

A quick scan of "teacher-twitter", or Edu-Twitter, as it has become known, will show there is a really strong emphasis on cognitive science and theories of learning. Numerous training courses, conferences, and books exist, which helpfully explore ideas around cognitive load, long-term memory, and other theories that are increasingly impacting the pedagogy we see in many classrooms and curriculum designs. Yet, as a sector, we are still remarkably quiet about what inevitably has a greater impact on the young people sitting in the classrooms: their psychological safety and a clear, detailed understanding of what is happening in their emotional brain.

Global studies have shown that in 2016 over 50% of children had experienced some form of violence in a 12-month period (Hillis et al., 2016). In 2020, WHO (the World Health Organization) estimated that one billion children aged 2–17 had experienced abuse; whether that be physical, sexual, emotional, or neglect. These children sit in front of our nation's teachers, but only a small number of our nation's teachers are trained to understand the impact such experiences will have had on their developing brains. The most contemporary neuroscience is showing us time and time again that stress in a child's life impairs the normal development of their brain and also of their entire nervous system. The amygdala, hippocampus, and prefrontal cortex, all areas of the brain that are vital in learning and self-regulation, are the key areas affected. It has been found that repeated exposure to stress early in a child's life can impact the functioning of the HPA (hypothalamic–pituitary–adrenal, key to managing stress), leading to children who are consistently on high alert to perceived threats (Butler et al., 2017). Scientists have shown that since 2014 children who have experienced stress and childhood trauma are more likely to internalise their feelings, leading to higher incidences of anxiety and depression. They are also more likely to suffer from low self-esteem. Unfortunately, these are sometimes the children who are most misunderstood in the education system. Many of us have heard, anecdotally, of children who have missed large chunks of school due to anxiety and have then been placed into an isolation room for having incorrect footwear, or for refusing to follow what *seemed* like a simple request from a teacher. How would schools look and what would they feel like, if as much emphasis was put into emotional psychological education, as has currently been going into cognitive science education?

All of the above thoughts, experiences, arguments, and calls for change will be explored in detail throughout this book. We will continually draw on the views, ideas, and experiences of the children and young people we have

Introduction

worked with over many years, and those gained through the various projects we have conducted over the past five years.

Summary

Through a series of chapter topics, we hope to present some of the key current challenges in the UK education system, and consider where such issues have come from in terms of the pedagogy and underpinning psychological theory. Through problem analysis we then aim to "rethink" ideas with workable solutions that are based on evidence, modern psychological theory, and neuroscience. Most importantly, we will incorporate the views of those currently learning and working in the system, both through research and work on the ground, using case examples to highlight some of the key challenges with current practice.

References

Butler, O., Herr, K., Pitman, R., Lesch, K.-P., Miller, C., and Gallinat, J., 2017. Child abuse, neural structure, and adolescent psychopathology: A retrospective study. *Neuroscience & Biobehavioral Reviews*, 73, pp. 456–471.

Department for Education (DfE), 2024. Children missing education. Available at: https://explore-education-statistics.service.gov.uk/find-statistics/children-missing-education/2024-25-autumn-term.

Hillis, S., Mercy, J., Amobi, A., and Kress, H., 2016. Global prevalence of past-year violence against children: A systematic review and minimum estimates. *Pediatrics*, 137(3), pp. e20154079.

National Institute for Health and Care Excellence (NICE) 2022. Social, emotional and mental wellbeing in primary and secondary education. Available at: https://www.nice.org.uk/guidance/ng223.

Popoola, M. and Sivers, S., 2023. Pupil views research: Children's perspectives on school and mental health. Unpublished internal report.

United Nations, 1989. Convention on the Rights of the Child. Available at: https://www.unicef.org.uk/what-we-do/un-convention-child-rights/.

World Health Organization, 2020. Child maltreatment. Available at: https://www.who.int/news-room/fact-sheets/detail/child-maltreatment.

1

Staff wellbeing and mental health

Putting on your oxygen masks first

Louise McDonagh

> I'm a person who likes to be as organised . . . proactive as possible . . . The first half term . . . has taken all of that away from me. I felt quite exposed. Quite vulnerable.
>
> School DSL and Year Leader

It can sometimes be difficult to imagine what it feels like to work in a challenging school, or any school in all honesty, unless you have been there and done it. It has to be said that all schools feel different, and every individual school feels different for each of the staff entering the building early every morning. One thing many staff will no doubt have in common, though, is a feeling that their work is not as respected as it may have been in years gone by, especially for those who have been in the profession for a number of years. The occupation of teacher has had somewhat of an image problem in recent years, which goes some way to explaining the falling number of graduates signing up to complete their PGCE (postgraduate certificate in education) or SCITT (school-centred initial teacher training). There is a deepening teacher shortage, and "golden hellos" have recently been updated and repackaged in a new guise aimed at retaining staff beyond their first few years in an attempt to reduce the flow of teachers out of the system (approximately 9.6% left the state sector in 2023 according to school workforce census data). These incentives are getting more generous in particular subjects, where the talent pool has become more of a shallow puddle. A couple of examples include £3,000 to £6,000 to teach chemistry, computing, mathematics, and physics, subjects which have always struggled to recruit when salaries are so much higher in the private sphere for graduates in these areas. The DfE (Department for Education) pushed the rewarding career angle, with their feel-good "Get into teaching" adverts for a number of years, resulting in many a rolled eye from current teachers who watched the teacher leaving at the same time as his pupils at the end of the school day! It is clear there is a problem, but how have we ended up here and what could be done to rectify this?

The reality on the ground

Firstly, we need to acknowledge that working full-time in a school is hard work. This seems reasonable but is at odds with the public perception of the profession. Hugh Gundlach is an education researcher at the University of Melbourne. One of his works was creating the Teachers on Screen Project (n.d.). His database of depictions of teachers on screen found that negative portrayals were more common than positive, inspiring representations of the role. He found teachers were often shown as lonely, lazy, boring, and even abusive characters. Similarly, Kim et al. found in their 2023 research that the Covid-19 pandemic exacerbated pre-existing issues that affected people's perceptions of teaching, including "continuous government disrespect" and "media vitriol towards teachers". It seems that it's not unreasonable for some school staff to feel defeated before they even step over the threshold. Oftentimes, the misunderstanding of what is involved in working in a school has no ill intent at all, but is based around a long-standing perception that teachers work short hours and have incredible holidays, too. I often wonder if because we have all had experiences of being in school, and having both teachers we adored and others we detested, that school staff are often seen as "fair game"?

Once staff walk into the building (long before 9am!), the demands that they face every day seem to be growing exponentially as schools try to plug the gaps left by many years of cutbacks to social care, community services, and even services you wouldn't imagine could impact schools with their reduction or loss. If we take a moment to consider what a typical day may consist of, it's easy to understand why working in education has been acknowledged as an occupation with heavy cognitive load: 1,500 decisions each eight-hour work day (Klein, 2021). Most staff will begin with preparing their classroom and resources, which in many schools can involve faulty equipment, queues for reprographics, attending morning briefings, and attending to staff and parent emails that have landed in their inbox overnight. In a typical lesson they will then need to navigate any number of SEND (special educational needs and disabilities) demands, be responsive to emails still popping into their inbox from other staff and leadership requiring immediate responses, deal with low-level and sometimes high-level behaviour issues, and be consistently ensuring their teaching stays within school expectations in terms of content, style, and delivery (more of this to come). They may be on a break or lunch duty that day, so lunch might be eaten on the go, and a bathroom visit is squeezed in before going back to the classroom. After school there may be CPD (continuous professional development)/training sessions, a staff meeting, or just the regular end of day duties with phone calls to be made, emails to be mopped up, safeguarding referrals to be sent, and planning and marking for the next day. If a class has completed an assessment, that may entail marking 25-plus pieces of work before their next lesson; this will usually be completed at home. One survey of teachers in the USA found that on average teachers work an additional 15 hours outside of the classroom per week; most of this is unpaid (Merrimack College and EdWeek Research Center, 2022). It is no surprise that many staff feel close to burn out.

Many of us will recognise the day described above, but how and why has it got to this point? How is it that an occupation that has often been considered a vocation, with the ensuing connotations of being purpose-driven, becomes an occupation that the NASUWT (teaching union) found had a wellbeing score of 38.4, significantly below the mean for the UK of 50–52. Of respondents in their 2023/2024 Wellbeing Survey Report, 86% reported that their job had adversely impacted their health. We often tell staff that they need to put their own oxygen mask on before they can effectively and compassionately support the most vulnerable children they work with, but how is this useful advice when they are struggling to find their own oxygen mask, or feel like it's not even available to them?

An issue that is consistently raised by school staff is the overbearing and somewhat childlike procedures and expectations placed on them by well-meaning leadership teams; sometimes placed on the senior leadership team (SLT) by academy executives and central teams. For example, many schools still insist that classwork is marked in a particular colour pen and that students also respond in a particular colour pen, with no evidence base that this improves learning or culture. Others will also insist that feedback follows a specific format, regardless of the subject and/or key stage. Some schools insist that every lesson follows a specific layout, with school logos on the resources and PowerPoint slides. Staff have reported being challenged by leaders in their classroom if a student has bracelets or earrings on, and warned that they are not upholding uniform expectations within the school. Policies in many schools are often beautifully presented documents, which do little to impact what is happening in the classrooms and corridors for students and staff alike. How often are these policies co-produced and how frequently is student or staff voice merely a tick-box exercise? One medium-sized academy chain in the Midlands decided in 2023 that all the departments across its varied schools would follow the same schemes of work, regardless of their context, their students, or their needs. Staff concerns (and justifiable anger) were ignored. These are just a small number of anecdotes, shared with or experienced first-hand by the authors, but they are certainly not unique.

Stephen Waters' (2021) fantastic book exploring staff wellbeing, found that there were 11 factors school staff identified as contributing to effective organisations:

1. Removal of high stakes accountability
2. Ensuring a creative and inspirational environment is developed and maintained
3. Understanding there can be no pupil wellbeing without staff wellbeing
4. Creating a culture of enablement
5. Encouraging staff to take risks without fear of failure
6. Introducing learning and study lessons/CPD
7. Introducing teacher research groups
8. Encouraging open lesson/classroom cultures
9. Acknowledging there is no "one way" of teaching
10. Removal of onerous data drops
11. Rejecting negative beliefs about staff and the school

None of these are surprising, or groundbreaking. What we see in these responses is a desire to work in an environment that removes strict hierarchical policies, for example, in lesson observations and didactic marking policies; an environment that embraces trust and belief in staff; encourages their development and respects their experience and professionalism. This means a full-scale rejection of what has become a predominant belief that the only way to raise standards is to monitor and inspect teachers and schools. A marginal gains approach to education has resulted in the removal of professionalism, creativity, trust, and respect. Waters (2021) found that in schools that have rejected these beliefs staff reported feelings of community, fairness, a connection to values, and greater reward from their work. Happy and motivated staff are more productive and positive.

As alluded to previously, schools have progressively become community hubs, plugging many of the gaps left for families as a result of years of austerity. Many schools introduced new roles within their pastoral teams with a focus on safeguarding, community liaising, and cohesion. For schools without any flexibility in their budgets, particularly those in more rural areas, staff have increasingly had to juggle these additional expectations and obligations alongside their usual heavy workload. Many pastoral teams and pastoral roles, especially in smaller secondaries and many primaries, are facilitated by teachers who perhaps receive a small TLR (teaching and learning responsibility payment – additional payments for school staff when they take on specific whole school responsibilities) and a few hours reprieve from their timetable. In addition to the workload issues, the emotional toll such roles have on individuals often goes unrecognised. Staff up and down the country are much more likely to have a good understanding of what Adverse Childhood Experiences (ACEs) are and the impact they can have on children, into adulthood. Many staff will even have been encouraged to fill in an ACEs questionnaire themselves at some point in a safeguarding training session (with very little consideration of the traumatic impact this might have for some of these staff). There is a much better understanding of the impact trauma and ACEs can have on the students in our care. However, very little is currently done to ensure staff themselves are adequately trained and supported to work with children with high ACE scores. Some schools will have at least four or five DSLs (Designated Safeguarding Leads), some who have been in the role for many years, dealing with the secondary trauma of working with vulnerable children and their families. The work these DSL teams do is excellent and intrinsic to a school's mission, but how many of those DSL teams have adequate support or supervision to help them deal with the compassion fatigue and vicarious trauma that come along with the DSL role? Staff in these roles have talked about the overload and burnout that can result from the constant feeling of being on high alert: "Everyone is just exhausted, and you see it. You see it in behaviour and stuff" (Staff member).

It is very easy to identify the problems school staff face in their day-to-day work, but it is more difficult for leaders to know what to do about this. Wellbeing has become somewhat of a buzzword in recent times and has become a footnote in many SLT meetings up and down the country. Undeniably there are leaders who hold this at the core of every decision they make and every new policy introduced, and they really consider the impact of changes on their staff community. Even then, a culture of wellbeing can be difficult to develop and sustain, especially if the school requires rapid improvement. It is also worth noting here that being the Headteacher/Principal can often be a lonely and difficult role. Too often, Heads and senior leaders will absorb the stresses and frustrations of their staff and have nowhere else to go with this emotional load. It makes me wonder: who can they turn to at the end of a long week, after the last teacher has just offloaded their frustrations or problems?

A step in the right direction

One significant improvement and development in recent years is the introduction of the Senior Mental Health Lead (SMHL) role in schools. The DfE's 2017 green paper on supporting children and young people's mental health had the ambition and aim that every school would have a trained SMHL in role by 2025. Whilst this was primarily focused on improving the mental health of children both in and out of school (data showed that school staff are the primary people that children turn to for help with their mental health needs), there was a promising and timely acknowledgement that schools needed a holistic, whole school approach to mental health, which also incorporated the mental health and wellbeing of staff. The training was delivered by DfE-approved facilitators, with the course audited periodically by the DfE to ensure the quality and efficacy. Schools were offered a £1,200 grant to cover some of the time and costs of a member of staff being released from school to attend the training. In Nottingham City and Nottinghamshire, as an example, 120 schools had been trained by the start of 2023. Many of the trained SMHLs audited their schools and identified ways to support both students and staff and started to implement plans to improve the overall environment within their schools. The DfE got a lot right in their roll-out of the scheme. However, feedback to SMHL training providers often had one theme: time and positionality. In the ever-demanding environment of a school, focus on the work that being a SMHL entails was often falling down the priority list. It often felt to many of the SMHLs that there wasn't enough time given to them by their line manager to effectively fulfil the role and it was merely tagged on to their existing job description. Furthermore, whilst the DfE recommended that the role was fulfilled by someone on the senior leadership team, often support staff were being chosen for the training. These staff often have some of the most important relationships with students (especially with the most vulnerable), but they were reporting that it was difficult to get support for meaningful change when they were not part of the leadership team, and didn't have the authority to assert the importance of the role. Schools need to consider who in their leadership team can take on this additional role, to ensure the SMHL doesn't become a footnote in action planning.

Supervision of key staff

Some schools are starting to recognise the value and importance of supervision. This is not the supervision of a line lead asking what you have achieved that week and if everything is okay generally, but a version of clinical supervision that many of the caring professions have as a matter of course: social workers, therapists, and many in mental health and medical fields. There is a growing movement towards providing SENCOs (special educational needs co-ordinators) and DSLs with regular supervision in schools, which suggests a welcome recognition of the need for additional support some roles in schools may require.

Supervision is different to line leadership in that there is less of a focus on operational efficiency and performance management and a greater focus on professional development, skill improvement, and emotional support. Supervision is not counselling but there is often a desire for the supervisee to process emotions that have come up in casework and situations; it is about unpacking the emotional labour involved in the supervisee's role, rather than counselling them through the emotions themselves. However, having said that, in my own experiences of delivering supervision, for some DSLs the first session has been an emotional offload; a release of months (sometimes years!) of dealing with trauma, hurt, and neglect. For some of my supervisees, this had been their first ever opportunity to talk about their role and their experiences in a way that wasn't about constant improvement or problem-solving, or that had an operational focus. DSLs, in particular, are often so acutely aware they are working with human beings, but they often forget they are humans, too, with needs and emotions.

In the busy and hectic world of a DSL or SENCO, there is often little time or space to discuss specific cases that have been challenging, unusual, or distressing; it is often 'onto the next'. In my own more than decade-long turn as a DSL, I dealt with a number of children being taken into care, police chasing my students down the street, children running away when it has all become too much, and even children dealing with the murder of a sibling. Some of the ICPCs (Initial Child Protection Conference) and Strat meetings involved hearing distressing and sometimes shattering information about children you cared about. Some of the disclosures I received from students still play over in my mind many years down the line. There was no specific support for me or the other DSLs, and so I would either go straight to teach my next lesson from these meetings or go home and stare at the TV screen to unwind. Regular supervision offers that time and space to reflect on the decision-making processes: what was successful, what was challenging, and what different support strategies could have been tried in these situations. They also offer the opportunity to consider what development the supervisee needs, with support and direction from someone who is usually more experienced than they are, but not necessarily senior to them. Barnardo's Scotland (2020) conducted a review into the use of supervision in schools in 2020 and found that the majority of staff were left feeling "supported but challenged". Of those surveyed, 33% were classroom teachers. One respondent shared that their supervision was an:

> Excellent opportunity to have a safe, confidential space to share concerns and successes and to be challenged and supported to understand my role in making progress and also how I can take next steps to success when things are confusing if less positive. This monthly Supervision has been a really essential part of my professional life and I now insist on all the people I manage having Supervision from others trained to do this effectively.

Another respondent talked about the impact on their emotional wellbeing: "Supervision is a most valuable process that gives everyone involved a voice. A safe space to talk honestly about what is happening and how you are feeling. I found it had a unique impact on my wellbeing."

There was some negative feedback, though, mainly focused on the difficulty of finding a time and keeping it clear in the busy environment of a school. One other critique was the impact that was felt when the supervision was treated as a tick-box exercise when conducted by a member of leadership who had received inadequate training. With 95% of the respondents saying they supported the principle of supervision in education, it begs the question: why is it not yet an enshrined part of a school's calendar, in much the same way that parent/carer conferences, line leadership meetings, department meetings, and the like are scheduled in as untouchable time? It is telling that I never missed a line leadership meeting that was in my calendar in all of my years in schools, but I noticed many of my supervisees often had to contact me to rearrange supervision because something had come up. I hope one day we prioritise the wellbeing and mental health of our staff as much as we prioritise holding them to account.

Education Psychology teams have offered this type of support to schools, usually as part of paid-for packages that are negotiated by schools, for a number of years, but many schools have simply not been aware of the offer, not been able to afford to cover the cost of ongoing supervision, or felt their small budget for Educational Psychology support needed to be spent on specific students. The NSPCC (National Society for Prevention of Cruelty to Children), University College London, and Tavistock and Portman NHS Trust are offering training to school staff to ensure someone in their team is capable of delivering supervision. Whilst this is a huge step in the right direction, schools need to be mindful of training staff who are in positions of authority and who may have line leadership responsibility of the people they are going to supervise. This structure can sometimes be unavoidable, but in some circumstances can impinge on the free and open discussion that supervision requires between the supervisor and supervisee. One final quote from the Barnardo's report (2020) so accurately sums up the belief at the start of this chapter:

> It seems to be a no-brainer to me! Educators are constantly supporting the mental health of those they are educating (and often their colleagues too) and this can be to the detriment of their own mental health. We need to be open and upfront about this, and if we really want to support young people to normalise mental health, then we need to be able to model this ourselves.

If we want our educators to put on their oxygen masks first, we need to provide them the time, space and ability to do this and maybe even give them the mask itself!

Leading with compassion

School leaders really do get a hard press! I have been a school leader and so have had to take on the chin some of the vitriol and criticism that is often thrown our way, sometimes justifiably. What is clear is that in some schools there has developed a feeling of mistrust between the leadership team and the staff they are meant to be inspiring and developing. Where has this crept in from? How can it be changed? How can we make this very challenging role in a school more sustainable for both the leader themselves (Headteacher burnout is a real and worrying phenomena) and the people they work with?

It would be very easy for this part of the book to become a poison-pen dedication to all of the leaders who are not doing it well and creating so much stress and anxiety for school staff, but we need to stop for a moment and reflect. Nobody has gone into school leadership for the dizzying salary, limitless power, and easy lifestyle! Nearly every leader wants their school to be the best; wants their students to be happy and achieving well; and wants to be respected by their teams. We do, however, need to examine some of the poor practices we are increasingly seeing and reflect on how we can change these for the better.

One experienced Headteacher shared with me his own feelings of frustration, surrounding his own micro-management by an Executive Head:

> Poor leadership has an impact on wellbeing that cannot be underestimated. As an employee who works hard and wants children to do well, all I want is to be recognised and acknowledged for my hard work. What's particularly disappointing with poor leadership is when leaders fail to acknowledge success as a team effort (and who simply use the outcomes as a self-celebration).
>
> Senior leader

This is an issue that can run all the way to the top, to Executive and CEO level. Other staff shared with me the biggest frustration from leadership is not feeling heard, or worse, feeling ignored:

> I was on the wellbeing committee for two years. Surveys were conducted and staff were asked what would help their wellbeing the most. The wellbeing initiatives that were put into place were nothing that staff had asked for. Even after a scathing organisational survey, SLT still worked to put a positive spin on the results, rather than actually listening to teachers.
>
> Staff member

We could fill ten pages with other experiences like this, but the picture is clear and doesn't need over-emphasising. There are bright spots and there are leaders who are getting it so right:

> On the positive side, no teacher is ever required to stay after 4pm (meetings are done on early dismissal days only). Professional development opportunities are extraordinary, [the LA] offers many courses that can be done virtually or in-person and teachers are urged to take part in this . . . Most staff feel valued and heard, as SLT has an open-door policy and conversations are constant; there is a real community feel that everyone feels part of.
>
> Staff member

Deci and Ryan's Self-Determination Theory (1985, 2000) offers a very succinct explanation for what works and what can go so terribly wrong in some schools. Deci and Ryan posit that human beings are motivated by three fundamental psychological needs:

1. **Autonomy:** feeling in control
2. **Competence:** feeling capable
3. **Relatedness:** feeling connected to others

When all three are present, humans feel intrinsically motivated and function in an optimal way. When one or more are missing, things can start to fall apart. Let's consider how much autonomy, for example, the average class teacher has in their room, or in their subject area. How many choices as a teacher do you have over the content you teach? Are you able to be creative?

Often the curriculum has been decided, to some extent by external forces such as exam boards and now, possibly, also by a MAT (multi-academy trust) curriculum team. The way that a lesson looks is often prescribed by the leadership team. The way that the day works is confined by timetable restrictions. What CPD a staff member gets access to can be confined by the school's calendar of training and what is deemed to be the school's and even the individual's most important needs. (According to whom is another question!)

Coming back to that pesky CPD, it can often be decided at the start of the year in a meeting with a line manager what a staff member's career targets for the year will be. There can be little room for manoeuvre or divergence from these targets as the year progresses due to rigid accountability measures for staff at all levels in the system. Do I feel competent if I have failed to meet my target because my (or my students') priorities changed? Do I feel competent in my role if every lesson observation has to have a development or next steps, regardless of how great the lesson might have been? Will a member of the team feel competent in their role if they are never encouraged to stretch themselves or their expertise and knowledge of other areas is never drawn upon? Leaders, how well do you know the strengths and abilities of your team? And how are you utilising opportunities to further develop your teams?

Regarding relatedness, the picture is even more concerning. For some staff, particularly primary teachers, you may go for many hours, often most of the day, without meaningful contact with other adults. No, meetings don't count either! How do I feel related to my colleagues if I'm catching up on my to-do list at lunchtime, or on duty in the cafeteria, or shovelling some food into me, before heading back to the classroom?

It is incumbent on schools, and specifically leadership teams, to find ways to improve these three psychological needs. It could be that the school employs more lunchtime supervision to ensure some protected time for staff to eat, unwind, and talk properly. Budgets are tight, so cost-free things include co-production of policies, and seeking ideas from staff at the early, planning stages of a new project. Audit your staff to find out what they have done before, what they know, what is it they love, and where can we utilise that in your school? A colleague of mine, who was part of the Citizens UK charity, introduced me to the concept of "rounds" before starting any meeting. This could be as simple as "where would you be, if you didn't have to be at work today?", which was answered by everyone in the meeting. Or "what is one thing that was really great about today?" – it can be work-related or more personal, but the idea is to remember that every person in that meeting is a whole human with a life outside of the building; this is relatedness.

In their book *Compassionate Leadership* (2022), Rasmus Hougaard and Jacqueline Carter dedicate an entire chapter to 'Unlearn Management, Relearn Being Human'. What does this mean in the workplace? It means, in their words, that as a leader you recognise your role as "developing and enabling meaningful and trusting relationships". We are wired to connect with other humans; our brain's biology and circuitry show us this, but too often the workplace becomes a space with rigid hierarchies. Managers and leaders mistakenly think that professionalism is keeping your personal life disconnected from the workplace; following a script that has been approved by HR and many leadership courses. How can we see an employee as a fully rounded human, if we don't know the name of their partner, or how their child is getting on in their new school, or how their pet's surgery went at the weekend? Hougaard and Carter quote numerous CEOs and powerful leaders throughout their book, but one quote that is particularly powerful comes from Kiersten Robinson of the Ford Motor Company, who says: "When we allow space to talk about how we are feeling and the struggles we are facing, we create a greater sense of compassion and common humanity that in turn fosters a more positive and productive work environment".

Happy staff work harder. It's not complicated! We have all experienced working in a toxic school before, and the students end up knowing it; the parents do, too, and the school gets a reputation. It becomes a spiral.

This is a huge undertaking for any Principal, Headteacher, or Executive Head, and it's important we don't lose sight of their humanity, too. As mentioned previously, who are they able to turn to when things become heavy and the burden can feel too much? This is when the hierarchy starts to eat itself. Schools need to be places where all staff, at any time, can feel comfortable to show their vulnerability and ask for help.

Final thoughts

With the statistics mentioned at the opening of this chapter, with the staff leaving in droves, and with difficulties in recruitment becoming more acute, it is more important than ever to prioritise the wellbeing of all the humans in the school building. We need to ensure staff know where their oxygen mask is, and make sure it gives them enough rich oxygen when they need to put it on. And try to create environments where the mask is rarely required in the first place.

Key takeaways

1. The emotional toll of working in schools is underestimated and unsustainable: staff across a range of roles face relentless pressures, high cognitive load, and growing responsibilities – particularly pastoral and safeguarding work – without adequate emotional support or recognition. Burnout and emotional exhaustion are common and often unaddressed.
2. Systemic challenges and leadership practices are contributing to declining staff wellbeing: rigid accountability, performative wellbeing policies, and lack of autonomy have eroded professional trust and satisfaction. Staff feel disempowered and unheard, while leaders themselves often lack the support needed to manage their own wellbeing.
3. There is an urgent need for cultural and structural change in schools: initiatives like the Senior Mental Health Lead role and the

introduction of clinical-style supervision are promising, but underutilised. A shift toward compassionate, relational leadership that values human connection, autonomy, and emotional safety is critical to creating healthier school environments.

References

Barnardo's Scotland, 2020. Review of Supervision in Schools. Available at: https://www.barnardos.org.uk.

Deci, E.L. and Ryan, R.M., 1985. *Intrinsic Motivation and Self-Determination in Human Behavior*. New York: Plenum.

Deci, E.L. and Ryan, R.M., 2000. Self-Determination Theory and the facilitation of intrinsic motivation, social development, and well-being. *American Psychologist*, 55(1), pp. 68–78. https://doi.org/10.1037/0003-066X.55.1.68.

Department for Education (DfE), 2017. Transforming Children and Young People's Mental Health Provision: A green paper. Available at: https://assets.publishing.service.gov.uk/media/5a823518e5274a2e87dc1b56/Transforming_children_and_young_people_s_mental_health_provision.pdf.

Gundlach, H., n.d. Teachers on Screen Project. University of Melbourne.

Hougaard, R. and Carter, J., 2022. *Compassionate Leadership: How to Do Hard Things in a Human Way*. Boston, MA: Harvard Business Review Press.

Kim, J., Ko, Y., Kim, W., Kim, G., Lee, J., Eyman, O.T.G., Chowdhury, S., Adiwal, J., Son, Y. and Lee, W.K., 2023. Understanding the impact of the COVID-19 pandemic on the perception and use of urban green spaces in Korea. *International Journal of Environmental Research and Public Health*, 20(4), p. 3018.

Klein, A. 2021, 6 December. 1,500 decisions a day (at least!): How teachers cope with a dizzying array of questions. *Education Week*. Available at: https://www.edweek.org/teaching-learning/1-500-decisions-a-day-at-least-how-teachers-cope-with-a-dizzying-array-of-questions/2021/12.

Merrimack College and EdWeek Research Center, 2022. 1st Annual Merrimack College Teacher Survey: 2022 Results. Available at: https://guinote.wordpress.com/wp-content/uploads/2024/02/merrimack_teachers_are_deeply_disillusioned_survey_data_confirms.pdf.

NASUWT, 2023/2024. Teacher Wellbeing Survey Report. Available at: https://www.nasuwt.org.uk.

Waters, S., 2021. *Cultures of Staff Wellbeing and Mental Health in Schools*. London: Open University Press.

2

Fear and rules

The views of children on the state of the current system

Louise McDonagh

> School rules are strict. I lose time learning, which is supposed to be the most important thing, for something stupid like talking in line.
>
> Child

The majority of people who decide they want to work in a school do so because they have a belief that education is a great leveller in society; that education provides the means to escape poverty, to overcome the barriers that still exist in racist, homophobic, sexist, and ableist societies around the world, as well as in the UK. One of Nelson Mandela's best-known quotations is "Education is the most powerful weapon which you can use to change the world". This thought and belief kept a fire burning in my belly for well over a decade working in some challenging contexts. I still love to be in the classroom with students, most recently teaching smart, articulate post-16 students Psychology. We debate, we share anecdotes, we think critically about research, headlines, and current events. However, I am acutely aware that for every classroom like that, there will be a student sitting in a booth somewhere else, with a booklet to learn from, for a uniform infringement or missing a detention. How on earth can we be okay with this? How can I be so sure this is happening? I know, because I wrote behaviour policies for a number of years, staffed isolation rooms and fully believed that without these robust (a euphemism for cold and callous) structures in place, the school would crumble. I continued to see this attitude, and *fear*, in other schools I visited around the city and county I worked in: "give them an inch and they'll take a mile".

The truth is that education as we know it, and have experienced it, is actually far from an egalitarian, uplifting mechanism. In fact, Augustina S. Paglayan argues in her richly researched book *Raised to Obey: The Rise and Spread of Mass Education* (2024) that throughout much of the world, the guiding idea behind developing primary education systems was to preserve the status quo within society. She argues that in the West, both sides of the political spectrum "agreed that the central goal of primary schools was to teach children obedience, discipline and good behaviour to support the stability of the state" (Paglayan, 2024, p. 17). This can be a difficult pill to swallow if, like me, someone entered the education system with aspirations to do the opposite: to encourage critical thinking, to break glass ceilings, and to make what John Lewis called "good trouble". However, a brief look at some of the most controversial and, unfortunately, increasingly widespread practices in schools (especially in the secondary sector) seems to support this premise. Behaviour points systems, isolation rooms/booths, and "flattening the grass" approaches all seem to suggest that children need to be treated with disdain, acute surveillance, and distrust. This is not to disparage any person working in a school where a "warm strict" approach is advocated, or to suggest that every child leaves those types of school traumatised, but it is to make us question the wider impact of such approaches and consider if we are ignoring a different approach, which is rooted in psychology and neuroscience.

"Flattening the grass" and punitive approaches

This idea became more widely known following the exposure of the practice in news outlets in 2019. They focused mainly on a small number of multi-academy trusts (MATs) where this approach seemed to be widespread. The idea was that shouting aggressively at pupils, as well as the use of "ritual humiliation", was encouraged by senior staff to instil discipline, particularly during the early stages of taking over a new school. This also included Executive Heads and Heads of School attending and leading assemblies or patrolling corridors, where students would be picked out for minor infringements and made an example of, at times until the child would cry. Leaders came forward at the time of the *TES* (*Times Education Supplement*) investigation to say they were trained in these approaches by visiting other schools within their trusts and taken on learning walks, to witness the grass being "flattened" first hand. It was alleged that staff were asked to identify their worst year groups so they could be seen and addressed first, and perhaps most aggressively. It is worth reiterating here that this was in 2019 – the 21st century! However, we seem to be enamoured in education of such systems, although perhaps less aggressive ones: house points and demerits.

Let's consider the widespread, almost universal use, of points-based behaviour systems; sometimes referred to as house points, negative points, consequences, or given a name that reflects the online system where they are being tracked. It is very rare indeed to find a school, both primary and secondary, where positive and negative points systems don't feature in the starring role of the school's behaviour policy. On the surface these systems can seem an effective, sensible, and efficient means to track behaviour, deal with negative behaviours, and reward the types of behaviour schools require to run safely. These systems can be traced back to the behaviourist approach of B.F. Skinner, one of the most famous psychologists of the 20th century. His research suggested that all human behaviour can be modified and shaped by either reinforcement ("You look so smart today, have a merit") or punishment ("You forgot your tie? Demerit for you, I'm afraid"). These principles were later adopted in schools in the 1960s, particularly in special education and behavioural units, using Applied Behaviour Analysis. These have morphed into our modern semblances with platforms like Class Dojo. They can and often do engage with elements of positive psychology to encourage growth mindset (Dweck 2006), and sometimes will be used hand in hand with restorative approaches. What's the problem with that, you ask? The main critique of this approach is the issue of compliance over understanding: *"I know I have to wear my tie to school or I'm in trouble, but I don't really understand why my school insists on this piece of uniform"*. Furthermore, research has shown that when implemented poorly, what can appear as a benign system can mirror punitive zero-tolerance approaches, which all disproportionately adversely affect Black students and students with SEND (Skiba et al., 2012). We convince ourselves that we are preparing our students for the world of work (where I have never once worn a tie!), when perhaps we are preparing them for the compliance Paglayan warned us about. In the stressful and busy environment of many schools, how often do we have the time to explain to students *why* their behaviour is not acceptable? With some of the rules a minority of schools insist on – silent corridors, only shoes beneath the ankle, banning of lip balm (seriously), or no tramlines in your hair (too extreme) – we have to wonder: have the adults even carefully considered the "why" at all? We are trying to develop positive behaviours through extrinsic means, rather than developing intrinsic motivation, which we will examine later in this chapter. While the tone here may be light-hearted, let's not underestimate the impact this can have on the young people the system is supposed to be supporting. One child in Popoola and Sivers' research commented: *"All that matters is that your uniform is correct and that your attendance is good"*.

A very recent example that was reported on in the media, as this book was nearing completion, is of a school that was sanctioning students who had shaved their heads, which is against the school's uniform policy. The students in question were told they could not attend their prom. Why would you shave your head just before the prom when you know it's against policy, you might ask. The answer: their friend (another student at the school) was going through chemotherapy treatment for cancer and they wanted to show their support in a meaningful and personal way. As one colleague so aptly commented: shouldn't this be commended rather than condemned?

Nobody enters the vocation of education to make a child feel that the only thing that matters is how they look in their uniform, but this is the message we are continually sending to our students, particularly those in the system who are most vulnerable: your learning is not as important as your compliance to the wider system. Points systems make some children feel they are a "good" student, and so conversely some feel they are a "bad" student. If I am a child who has not learnt how to regulate my own emotions, if I have lived in a chaotic household, or even one where my parents are simply too busy working to be present for me, sometimes I might not be able to follow all the rules. If I end up on the bottom cloud in my classroom, or if I find myself always on the amber or red traffic light, does that mean I'm inherently "bad"? If every other child in my class can see that, how am I meant to feel? This is the other problem with such systems: they inadvertently encourage public shaming. One of the students in Popoola and Sivers' research shared how these sorts of punitive and shaming approaches made them feel, in devastating simplicity: *"Always in trouble. Makes me feel like I'm a failure to my family. Makes me not want to be alive."*

Aside from the issues around the punishments associated with behaviour charts, the rewards are not always creating the desired outcome either. Alfie Kohn spent most of his career researching the impact of rewards on human behaviour, children and adult workers alike. In his seminal work *Punished by Rewards: Beyond Punishment* (1993), he argues convincingly that reward systems diminish our intrinsic motivation. For example, children who are rewarded for reading may read more at the beginning, as a desire for a reward is fresh and exciting, but may in fact read less over time as the reward becomes less tangible; which then becomes *"what is the point in reading if I'm not going to keep getting rewarded for it?"* rather than reading for the enjoyment of it. It also creates a transactional environment many of us have seen firsthand. Students begin to behave in ways that are deemed socially beneficial, but in the hope they'll be given house points by the teacher they held the door open for, or for whom they carried exercise books. We *hope* that these behaviours will eventually create a culture over time, or become learned habits, but I wonder how often that is the case? Surely relationships are what create these cultures in schools, rather than "token economies" (Kohn, 1993)? This brings us back to the idea of intrinsic motivation. If we are continually rewarding the behaviour we want to see, how are we encouraging and nurturing in students the desire to do something for its own sake?

Kohn argues there are alternatives to the behaviourist approach, and these have been shown to work across a variety of different types of school. He advocates for developing children's autonomy, mastery, and sense of purpose. It brings to mind one of my favourite quotes about education: "Education is not the filling of a pail, but the lighting of a fire" (W.B. Yeats). These might seem like lofty ideals, particularly if you are considering a Year 9 maths class last lesson of the day, or Year 3 after their lunch break. However, this does not need to be revolutionary! It can be small adaptations like giving students a choice of how they will be assessed on their most recent scheme of work; do they want to write a diary home from the trenches, or write a newspaper report about the trench experience? Encourage students to see struggle as part of the process of mastery; what Doug Lemov (yes, *some* of Teach Like a Champion is very trauma-aware!) refers to as creating a "Culture of Error". Every teacher knows what scaffolding looks like; this helps to create mastery, but sometimes we need to be explicit when telling students that. A science practical, for example, could focus less on getting the "correct" outcome and more on creating a hypothesis, testing it, maybe failing, and revising the approach. To create a sense of purpose, students need to also know the why behind the task: how is this improving their skills in the real world? What is the big picture behind learning this, other than "you need to know this for Paper 1 of your exam"? Lastly, allow students to sometimes set their own goals and self-reflect on their learning: "What do I think I did successfully in this piece of work?", as opposed to "What is my teacher telling me I did well?" This kind of reflection on learning isn't meant to replace the teacher as the expert, but encourages moments of self-reflection as a learner, and isn't that what education is about? It is interesting, but not surprising, to note the overlap between Kohn's recommended approach and Deci and Ryan's Self-Determination Theory (1985, 2000), which was discussed in Chapter 1. Perhaps motivating and making small humans happy is not as complicated as we sometimes think it is.

We do have to spend some moments exploring a more concerning and divisive aspect of the systems widely adopted in many schools: isolation. The last few years have seen a spotlight shone on schools' use and implementation of isolation rooms and, most controversially, isolation booths. In 2021 the British Psychological Society (BPS) called for an outright ban of isolation booths in UK schools. Whilst no ban has come to fruition at the time of writing, the current Labour government has shown signs and used rhetoric around reforming schools' use of such methods. We wait with bated breath. Where did booths come from and how did they gain such popularity, particularly in some secondary-based MATs?

I qualified as a teacher in 2005 and every school I have worked in, or visited, until very recently, has had some type of isolation facility; a space students are taken to if their behaviour has been deemed too egregious, dangerous, or disruptive to learning to consider keeping them in the classroom among their peers. In more recent years, they have been utilised as an alternative to sending a student home on a suspension (or what used to be known as a Fixed Term Exclusion). A few things that these spaces have often had in common are: they are not decorated nicely (usually purposefully); the child is not given a choice whether to be there or not and refusal will often escalate to a suspension; children are not permitted to talk to any other children in the room; work is often delivered via an online platform or work booklet. Only rarely is the member of staff in the isolation room qualified as an ELSA (Emotional Literacy Support Assistant), and even more rarely are they trained in trauma-aware and therapeutic approaches to working with dysregulated children. You could surmise that we are often creating the perfect storm for further dysregulation, and suspension, as well as unsupported and stressed staff. Some schools take the idea of isolation a step further by using boards or panels around the desks to create a booth. Some students will work in these booths for half a day, the whole day, or even multiple days in the most extreme cases. One such example is a child of 13, residing in the East Midlands, who is consistently isolated for her "poor" behaviour: mainly not attending a detention, or incorrect uniform: *"I've been staring at a wall all day"*.

Framing attendance as the golden ticket to educational success becomes meaningless when a small percentage of a school's students will sit with no teaching or instruction and participate in a minimal amount of learning.

Isolation rooms and booths arrived on the education scene in the late 1980s and early 1990s as a response to concerns about the rise in student behavioural issues. Staff did not feel equipped to deal with what they were seeing in the classroom, and so isolation rooms provided a temporary solution to the problem. Forty years later, we have become almost dependent on them as a strategy for punishing behaviour, when we perhaps need to spend more time thinking of strategies to change behaviour. Sealy et al. found in their 2021 research paper that there is limited research on the efficacy of isolation rooms as punishment, and yet we continue to use them with very little guidance or boundaries in how they can or should be used. They also found that different schools had different rationale for placing children in the isolation room in the first place, thereby making it difficult to determine if this form of exclusion (albeit internal) is "reasonable, fair and proportionate" (Department for Education [DFE], 2024). Sealy et al. (2021) describe the intense surveillance children experience in these rooms, something all three of the writers can attest to: lesson-by-lesson scrutiny of behaviour, often accompanied by escorted toilet breaks and monitoring of computer usage. Many of the rooms are even designed for optimum supervision at all times. Supervision of children is, of course, an important element of safeguarding, but are we doing this to support the children in isolation, or to unconsciously (or consciously) reassert the authority of the adults in the school and remind the children of who is in control? When we take a moment to step back and realise this is not about blaming school staff but considering how to do things differently, we can start to see the concept and practice of isolation rooms as scarily dystopian. This idea of control and authority is highlighted by one of the participants in Sealy et al.'s study, who shared the following:

> It's always, "Say sorry to the teacher". There's no ifs, buts, ands [pause] just say sorry to the teacher. There's been times when I've said, "I've never done it" and they'd say, "I know, I know but just say sorry to build a bridge".

This, again, brings us back to the idea of mass education as a means to control and teach obedience. If this is not the education system you recognise as your inspiration, or that you want to be part of, the question is: how can we do things differently?

Reimagining behaviour approaches

There is no quick fix and also no one-size-fits-all approach to the rules and systems that schools so obviously need in order to run efficiently and safely. However, there are some fundamental principles that run through all of the amazing schools, alternative provisions, and colleges that we three authors have visited throughout our careers. It's hard to put these principles into words, because it is more of a feeling or culture that runs through them like a message in a stick of rock. Most simply, though, it could be described as having a purpose over having power; a kindness that doesn't mean shying away from sometimes making really difficult decisions; and always treating students how you would want your own child to be treated. It is encapsulated in this thought-provoking quote from Dr Dan Siegel and Dr Tina Payne Bryson (2011): "Too often we forget that discipline really means to teach, not to punish. A disciple is a student, not a recipient of behavioural consequences." What does this look like on a practical level, and how can these principles inform the rules and systems we fall back on so easily and unquestioningly in the current education system?

Here is where I unashamedly, and with so much bias, introduce you, the reader, to my good friend and much missed colleague, Sam Chapman. Sam was ultimately, and tragically, taken far, far too soon by an aggressive and relentless cancer. She was the inspiration and the impetus for this book being written, and she also happened to run one of the most effective in-school alternative provisions I have seen. After her daughter, family, and partner, the provision was her pride and joy: Compass.

It was in 2020 that the local authority area I worked within was willing to give a small pot of money to secondary schools who signed up to their proposal to reduce permanent exclusions. The money was to be spent on inclusive measures that would reduce the number of children being permanently excluded from school, and hopefully also the number of suspensions (then referred to as Fixed Term Exclusions) at the same time. The proposal was not perfect, but it was a good symbolic and sensible step towards becoming a more inclusive city. My principal was supportive of us using the money we were given to build something in our school that was sorely needed; a provision for those students who found themselves trapped in the revolving door of exclusions, and also for those who maybe just found being in mainstream school too stressful sometimes. We interviewed for a provision lead in February 2020 and Sam stood out from everyone else we interviewed that day as the right person for the job. However, March 2020 came and with it the announcement of a national lockdown. It wasn't until the following academic year that we were able to start putting our plans for Compass into action and see them come to fruition. When I say "we", I had some vague ideas of what I wanted and our school needed, but it was Sam who went away and researched, planned, costed, and spent many sleepless nights wondering if it would work. A space in the school that was underutilised was repurposed, given some cosmetic work, and christened Compass.

Compass was envisioned as a place where students worked away from the distractions and tumult of their usual timetable. There was an onboarding process where families were invited to come and see the provision and students could hear what it was all about. For the provision to have any impact we needed the students' buy-in; they'd had so many choices and freedoms taken away from them previously that this could not be seen or perceived by them as a punishment. There was never to be discussions between the Head of Year and families or students where the dialogue resembled anything like "If your behaviour continues you will have to go into Compass". The students would follow their mainstream curriculum in the main, which was made easier by the whole school using lesson packets and detailed medium-term planning. However, if they had already identified areas where they felt successful or had a good relationship with the teacher, these were times of the day where they went back to their mainstream lessons and still felt connected to their peers and teachers. That connection was so important for their feelings of relatedness and the understanding that they would at some point reintegrate back into the mainstream. For some this would take much longer and would never be a full reintegration. The other parts of their curriculum involved learning life skills but also looking at Social Emotional Aspects of Learning (SEAL): how to regulate themselves, and how to notice when they were leaving the green zone to enter the amber or red zones – skills that if they didn't learn now could have dire consequences once they left secondary school. They also had regular access to the school counsellor (who had been trained and qualified as part of her career development by the school) as part of their curriculum. One of the most important elements of Compass, however, was the team around Sam. She interviewed, appointed, and curated a team who brought different perspectives, life experiences, and personalities. She trained all of them in restorative approaches and trauma-informed approaches, and she gave them the space and time to unpick incidents that had occurred in the day with their key students, to wonder about why something had happened.

A very simple process that was introduced was the Compass CAF. There may be some readers who remember the CAF (Common Assessment Framework) fondly; others maybe not so much! It was a tool used by schools as an early intervention before a child was referred to external agencies. It became the stuff of legend that a school's Designated Safeguarding Lead (DSL) would call their authority's social care helpline and be asked, "Have you initiated a CAF?" Your heart would sink; it was a very, very long process and the lead professional would often end up being a member of school staff. The Compass team adapted this paperwork and made it more relevant to their setting and more user-friendly. The child and their family were invited in to be a part of the process, and this was a way of really understanding what has happened in the child's life; we often miss so much of a child's background and events in their life that could help us to understand their behaviours and emotions a little more. A number of these Compass CAFs threw up information about parental incarceration, domestic abuse, and gaps in education, all of which built a much more nuanced picture of the child and how the world looked to them. This didn't need to involve external agencies and was treated with confidentiality and compassion. In the world of safeguarding, we often talk of "professional curiosity", but as classroom teachers, pastoral staff, or school leaders, that curiosity is just as important as any system we might create and roll out on an INSET (in-service education and training) day.

Every day in Compass brought its challenges, but it also brought stronger relationships between the students and their Compass team, relationships that they hadn't necessarily really experienced in mainstream lessons before. Suspensions dropped, time spent in the school's isolation room dropped (yes, it still had one of those . . . baby steps!), permanent exclusions were reduced, and attendance improved significantly for the students attending Compass. One of the first Compass students had a school attendance rate of 50% but managed to get her attendance up to over 80% in the first term of being in the provision. The students reported being happier, too. Happy students learn! A former staff member, Cornelius Ogunlade, shared his experience of working in Compass with me:

> What Sam created through Compass gave young people hope; a sense of direction. Sam transformed and empowered the lives of many young children who society was ready to give up on. Through Compass, the team was able to

holistically mentor and guide the lives of vulnerable young people, empowering them, showing them that it was possible to regain control: control of their future.

If all schools could find the will and the way to recreate this type of in-house provision, whether that is small-scale or whole-scale, perhaps we would see a higher level of engagement with school, lower levels of internal and external exclusions from education, and greater levels of wellbeing in our children.

One of the respondents in Popoola and Sivers' research said that "feeling part of something" made her feel happy in school. How can we try to make more students feel part of something more frequently? How can we find opportunities to make them feel seen and heard? This comes back to the Deci and Ryan (1985, 2000) concepts of relatedness and autonomy, crucial for psychological wellbeing. The students in Compass felt involved in their education, not unwilling and powerless participants. However, not every school has a budget that can stretch to creating a bespoke and discrete provision, so there are approaches that cost nothing and can transform a culture.

Why try trauma-informed approaches?

Trauma-informed approaches have become a divisive topic in the world of education – often due to a misunderstanding and mischaracterisation of what trauma-informed, sometimes called trauma-aware, actually means. This is not a book about trauma-informed approaches; there are some fantastic ones out there: Joe Brummer and Tom Brunzell are both excellent! We do want to leave you, however, with some practical ideas about how to start to replace fear- and shame-based systems, with those that are more kindness-led and often more effective in the long term. Trauma-informed means having an understanding of the impact childhood trauma can have on the development, reactions, and behaviour of children. It does not mean we "diagnose" or even try to act as a pro-bono therapist, as is often argued by people who are not in favour of a trauma-informed approach. It is about understanding the different ways trauma can manifest and recognising that quite often we do not know which of the children (or adults!) in our building may have suffered developmental trauma, and therefore we act accordingly – with grace and compassion.

Trauma-informed approaches to learning lean away from shaming students, and lean into relational approaches, which are explored more significantly in Chapter 3. This does not mean being *friends* with students, but it does mean being human in our interactions with children and young people. We can be authoritative, without being authoritarian. This approach also means all staff need to understand how a child's brain develops and what can impact on the development of a healthy brain. Furthermore, what might this then look like in the classroom?

One of the first sessions most staff will do when a school is moving towards a more relational approach is centred around a child's developing brain. It is important to understand the science, the *why* behind adopting such an approach, and the different types of trauma children can experience, and recognise the differences between fight, flight, freeze, and fawn. Staff in a trauma-informed environment will recognise that sometimes a child's reaction is not a choice; it is a survival response driven by their amygdala, which has become trained to see danger in places that, to us, don't seem dangerous at all. When we think a child has gone from zero to one hundred and it baffles us, that is their brain working to keep them safe.

Fight: yelling, screaming, swearing, physical assaults, defiance, "backchat".
Flight: running out of the classroom, hiding, spending time in the toilets or corridors, avoiding tasks, restlessness, or avoiding school altogether.
Freeze: going silent or non-verbal, daydreaming, staring blankly, head on the desk.
Fawn: being the helper or "model student", constantly aiming to please, avoiding any conflict at all costs.

If we think about the deep feeling behind each of the responses, it boils down to the same emotion or state: safety. Trauma-informed approaches involve finding ways to make the environment of school feel safe for children (and the adults), because we cannot engage our thinking brain, the cerebral cortex, if our feeling brain is on high alert all the time. It is also important to facilitate a culture shift where staff can start to recognise what their own trigger points might look like: *what happens to me, when I'm feeling dysregulated?*

Trauma-informed approaches, as a minimum, require:

- Clear boundaries
- Clear and consistent routines
- Strong relationships
- Modelling of regulation and co-regulation
- Co-production with staff, students, and home

For some schools, this can mean a complete sea change in approach and culture. For many, however, it requires reflecting on current practices and making tweaks to how things are implemented. Let's look at two strategies that have worked tremendously in a range of contexts and require nothing more than training, understanding, and willingness to make it work.

Emotion coaching

This strategy involves training staff and then training students to recognise their own emotions and how to manage them in different situations. It comes under the umbrella of SEAL or SEL (Social Emotional [Aspects] of Learning).

We know that the ability to manage our emotions and develop emotional resilience are important factors in securing academic success, as well as ensuring our general happiness and success navigating the world around us. Emotion coaching in schools was developed from Dr John Gottman's work on parenting styles (published in 1997, but based on more than a decade of work and research). It is a simple five-step approach that can be used with all ages of children and in all types of settings:

1. **Be aware of the child's emotions:** what might they be feeling in this moment? How might they be expressing it in their words or body language?
2. **Validate their emotion:** "It's okay to feel what you are feeling right now – I think I would feel that too".
3. **Name the emotion:** "I wonder if you're feeling angry or frustrated right now?", "I can see you're sad at the moment".
4. **Show empathy and understanding:** use active listening: "That sounds tough; I think I would feel angry too".
5. **Set boundaries and problem-solve together:** "We cannot shout at other students like that. So how can we fix this?"

Bath Spa University, in 2015, researched the impact of Emotion Coaching in both primary and secondary schools in the UK. They found that if staff felt better prepared to de-escalate incidents with children, the students were better able to regulate themselves and each other, and that there was a better culture of wellbeing developed as a result of the training and implementation of the approach. Neuroscience would seem to back this up; naming our emotions and feeling validated activates our prefrontal cortex (the logical and "thinking" part of the brain). It also helps to regulate our amygdala's stress response (the emotional and "fight–flight" part of the brain). When I have shared this training with staff, one piece of feedback I always know I am going to get is: "But this takes such a long time". Stop for a minute and think about how long that interaction could take in reality – maybe a minute and a half, two minutes maximum? If every member of staff takes that time to connect and work with the child's emotions, how many much longer, more negative conversations might we save ourselves? When I was a Head of Year, I often used to reflect on what a disproportionate amount of my time and resources were being spent on a small number of children; on how that time could have been used differently had I, and my colleagues, known about emotion coaching; and on how that time might not have been needed for those negative interactions if my students had been coached through these emotions throughout their school career.

Unconditional positive regard

Teachers who actually care.
Child

When asked the question, "What are your ideas about how school could be different, what would have made it easier for you/what would you need to be able to go back?", it is a little soul-destroying to see so many children respond with answers like the above: *"teachers who actually care"*; *"teachers who are more understanding"*; *"teachers who don't shout"* (Popoola and Sivers, 2024). No one goes into the education system with the intent to shout at children and make school a difficult experience for them, but it *is* happening. The psychologist Carl Rogers was one of the biggest proponents of the concept of Unconditional Positive Regard. It developed as a therapeutic approach, but has since evolved to become part of a wider therapeutic and trauma-informed approach in schools, which costs nothing to implement, other than time and patience.

Unconditional Positive Regard, at its heart, is about a person flourishing.; it's why many of us chose to follow a career path in the education system and work with children. In a school it looks like challenging a child's behaviour but always continuing to see them as a person that you care about and letting them know this. Of course, this is so much easier said than done, especially when a child knows which buttons of yours to press or has been very personal in a nasty comment towards you. This is not about accepting or ignoring negative behaviour. But when the child has done something wrong, we understand that the behaviour doesn't define them as a person; we still care about them, even if we might be disappointed at that moment in time. This can be as simple as changing the language we use around schools and in the classroom, where the focus becomes the behaviour rather than the child:

Instead of: "You are always rude to people"
Try: "That was really rude what you said just then, and I know you can do better than that".
Instead of: "Why are you shouting? Stop shouting!"
Try: "I can see you're really frustrated. What can I do?"

As mentioned previously, relatedness is so important to all of us as human beings, and showing that we will never withdraw our care or concern for a child as punishment is a big step towards building self-esteem, self-regulation, and emotional resilience. When we talk about modelling behaviour in schools, we can often mean not being on our mobile devices, or chewing gum, and talking politely. They are all important when developing a culture that is fair and equitable, but it is this kind of modelling of Unconditional Positive Regard-style responses that are most important if we want our students to be happy, self-regulating, and successful.

Final thoughts

There is no silver bullet when it comes to running a calm, orderly, and warm school environment. However, there are things we can work on straight away, and there are bigger considerations that require a wholesale rethink of what our education system is aiming to achieve, for whom, and why. That being said, as seen through the children's testimonies throughout, there is an urgent need for some of these changes to happen now. Many of these changes simply require a change in perspective to happen, first and foremost. As hopefully shown in this chapter, dismantling some of our draconian and questionable behaviour approaches and behaviour systems is something we could change just by opening our eyes, ears, and hearts to doing it differently.

Key takeaways

1. Behaviour systems in schools often prioritise compliance over connection, to the detriment of student wellbeing: approaches such as isolation booths, strict uniform rules, and points-based behaviour management systems can foster anxiety, shame, and disengagement – particularly among vulnerable learners. Children report feeling dehumanised and reduced to their level of compliance, rather than being seen as individuals.
2. There is a growing case for trauma-informed, relational practices that centre emotional safety: the chapter highlights the benefits of alternative approaches rooted in psychology and neuroscience, including emotion coaching and Unconditional Positive Regard. These strategies support regulation, belonging, and intrinsic motivation rather than relying on punitive or performative discipline. They also lead to better staff wellbeing as an additional outcome.
3. Examples of inclusive, compassionate provision show a way forward: case studies like Compass illustrate how schools can reduce exclusions and improve attendance and wellbeing by creating psychologically safe spaces, strong relationships, and individualised support. With vision and commitment – not necessarily large budgets – schools can reimagine discipline as a process of guidance, not punishment.

References

Brummer, J., 2020. *Building a Trauma-Informed Restorative School: Skills and Approaches for Improving Culture and Behavior.* London: Jessica Kingsley Publishers.

Brunzell, T. and Norrish, J., 2021. *Creating Trauma-Informed, Strengths-Based Classrooms: Teacher Strategies for Nurturing Students' Healing, Growth, and Learning.* London: Jessica Kingsley Publishers.

Deci, E.L. and Ryan, R.M., 1985. *Intrinsic Motivation and Self-Determination in Human Behavior.* New York: Plenum.

Deci, E.L. and Ryan, R.M., 2000. Self-Determination Theory and the facilitation of intrinsic motivation, social development, and well-being. *American Psychologist*, 55(1), pp. 68–78. https://doi.org/10.1037/0003-066X.55.1.68.

Department for Education (DfE), 2017. Transforming Children and Young People's Mental Health Provision: A green paper. Available at: https://assets.publishing.service.gov.uk/media/5a823518e5274a2e87dc1b56/Transforming_children_and_young_people_s_mental_health_provision.pdf.

Department for Education (DfE), 2024. Suspension and Permanent Exclusion Guidance. Available at: https://assets.publishing.service.gov.uk/media/66be0d92c32366481ca4918a/Suspensions_and_permanent_exclusions_guidance.pdf.

Dweck, C.S., 2006. *Mindset: The New Psychology of Success*. New York: Random House.

Gottman, J. M. and DeClaire, J., 1997. *Raising an Emotionally Intelligent Child: The Heart of Parenting*. New York: Simon & Schuster.

Gus, L., Rose, J. and Gilbert, L., 2015. Emotion coaching: A universal strategy for supporting and promoting sustainable emotional and behavioural well-being. *Educational & Child Psychology*, 32(1), pp. 31–41.

Hazell, W., 2019a, 8 February. Exclusive: Outwood Grange uses "crisis managers" to explain "flattening the grass" policy. *TES Magazine*. Available at: https://www.tes.com/magazine/archive/exclusive-outwood-grange-uses-crisis-managers-explain-flattening-grass-policy.

Hazell, W., 2019b, 26 February. Exclusive: "Flattening the grass" is "frightening to watch", say new sources. Available at: https://www.tes.com/magazine/archive/exclusive-flattening-grass-frightening-watch-say-new-sources.

Kohn, A., 1993. *Punished by Rewards: The Trouble with Gold Stars, Incentive Plans, A's, Praise, and Other Bribes*. Boston, MA: Houghton Mifflin.

Kohn, A., 1998. *Punished by Rewards: The Trouble with Gold Stars, Incentive Plans, A's, Praise, and Other Bribes* (2nd ed.). Boston, MA: Houghton Mifflin.

Lemov, D., 2010. *Teach Like a Champion: 49 Techniques That Put Students on the Path to College (K–12)*. New York: John Wiley & Sons.

Paglayan, A., 2024. *Raised to Obey*. Princeton, NJ: Princeton University Press.

Popoola, M. and Sivers, S., 2024. Young people's views on mental health: School is too much pressure. edpsy.org.uk. Available at: https://edpsy.org.uk/blog/2024/news-school-is-too-much-pressure-young-people-identify-school-as-a-contributing-factor-to-poor-mental-health/.

Sealy, J., Abrams, E.J., and Cockburn, T., 2021. Students' experience of isolation room punishment in UK mainstream education. "I can't put into words what you felt like, almost a dog in a cage". *International Journal of*

Inclusive Education, 27(12), pp. 1336–1350. https://doi.org/10.1080/13603116.2021.1889052.

Siegel, D.J. and Bryson, T.P., 2011. *The Whole-Brain Child: 12 Revolutionary Strategies to Nurture Your Child's Developing Mind*. New York: Delacorte Press.

Skiba, R.J., Shure, L., and Williams, N., 2012. Racial and ethnic disproportionality in suspension and expulsion. In A.L. Noltemeyer and C.S. Mcloughlin (Eds.), *Disproportionality in Education and Special Education* (pp. 89–118). Springfield, IL: Charles C. Thomas.

UK Government, 2024, August. Suspension and permanent exclusion from maintained schools, academies and pupil referral units in England, including pupil movement. Available at: https://assets.publishing.service.gov.uk/media/66be0d92c32366481ca4918a/Suspensions_and_permanent_exclusions_guidance.pdf.

3

Relationships, relationships, relationships

Sarah Sivers

Going to school and connecting with my friends really helps me and i enjoy it but i do think we don't get enough time to do so at all [sic].

Child

Reflection point

Here are a few questions for you to consider before we explore the thoughts and experiences children and young people shared about relationships:

- "What are your key memories about school and how are relationships involved with these memories?"
- "Are there any teaching staff that you remember in particular? Why is this?"

A theme that threaded through all the research we carried out with children and young people is the importance of relationships (Popoola and Sivers, 2021, 2023; Sivers et al., 2022). These relationships encompass family, friends, school staff, people in the wider community, and even pets. The children and young people told us incredibly moving stories about the people they cared about and who cared for them. However, they also provided insights into how painful it could be to experience separation from the people they cared about, particularly during the lockdown periods.

Children and young people also shared less-positive experiences connected to relationships: the difficult experiences of falling out with friends, family or school staff; experiences of bullying (in-person and online); feeling like they didn't belong; and having a sense of isolation and sadness, which they felt before, during, and after the lockdown periods.

These experiences are brought to life in the next section as we explore what the children and young people told us.

What the children and young people said ... about relationships

The children and young people mentioned the importance of relationships across all age ranges and across all the research we conducted. It was a constant theme, which also overlapped with other themes, such as home and school experiences and mental health, and connected to a sense of safety. Below we will explore some of these themes and share the children and young people's words to provide insights into the importance and complicated nature of relationships.

Family and friends

It was very moving to read how many children and young people enjoyed being with their family during lockdown, but also missed their friends. Throughout our research the importance of relationships with others was mentioned:

- *"I miss everyone but I am happy being at home learning with mummy."*
- *"Seeing friends and seeing family is incredibly important."*
- *"My friends have this incredible way of making my heart happy and complete, I love them so much <3."*

Experiences of difficulties in friendships and bullying

The children and young people also shared experiences of more negative relationships, particularly with peers. There were sadly many children who shared experiences of difficulties within friendship groups and bullying (in-person and online). There was a clear distinction between the difficulties that arose within friendship groups (falling out and "drama") and the experience of being bullied. There was also another strand that spoke of isolation, not being noticed by anyone in either a positive or negative way:

- *"I think there needs to be more support for children who are lonely and have no friends."*
- *"I feel less comfortable around my friends than before."*
- *". . . managing the worries of staying safe from Covid-19, as well as impact of bullies."*

Teaching staff

Positive and negative relationships with teaching staff was also something the children and young people shared. The thoughts shared by primary school children were on the whole more positive, compared with secondary-aged young people. However, there are a number of factors to explain this: we need to take into account that the relationships are different in primary school, often with a small number of teaching staff seeing a class through an academic year. In addition to having many more teachers in secondary school, this is also a developmental stage where young people are seeking more autonomy, which can push against rules and expectations in school. However, what seems to be important is a sense of safety and being understood. This complexity is highlighted in the following children's quotes:

- *"I feel safe at school because there are lots of staff around at all times . . . there is always a teacher checking on everyone."*
- *"My tutor helped me when I returned to school after the first lockdown as I suffer with anxiety which develops into panic attacks."*
- *"The teachers are scary, always stressed and shouting."*

Dynamic and shifting relationships

What really interested us when reading the words of the children and young people was the way many of them saw and experienced things in multifaceted ways. Many of the shared thoughts showed two sides of an experience, the dark and the light – an ability to see things from different perspectives. One child said: *"Friendship is a good thing for me but also it is very easy for me to go wrong with friendship and end up being bullied or hurt by any of my old friends"*.

The insights the children and young people provided, about the positive and negative aspects of relationships, demonstrate the central role relationships play in all areas of their lives. If a child or young person feels a sense of belonging, care, and connection, this can have a profound impact on their lives, sense of self, and, specifically to education, the way they engage with and enjoy learning. This is the case for all children and young people, but even more so for those who may not have had consistent experiences of belonging, care, and connection. It is also important to keep in mind that belonging, care, and connection are important for the adults, and this is why the concept of relational approaches can revolutionise the way education is structured.

Relational approaches

The belief that relationships are important in education has long been on the periphery of pedagogy, with "behaviour management" approaches at the centre. The concept of relational approaches is becoming more prevalent in education. However, these approaches are often seen as an intervention for those requiring additional support, rather than a guiding ethos. There is often scepticism about the power of relationships within schools as an agent for meaningful change, with more traditional forms of behaviour management being used as a preferred approach. This has resulted in two camps, with increasingly polarised views on the suitability (or not) of either approach.

Why is this the case and how can we shift thinking to encompass the beneficial elements of both?

We should not be "doing" relational approaches for certain groups or individuals; it should be embedded into the fabric of the school ethos and day, across all educational settings. Relational approaches are beneficial for all – children, young people, and adults. But what do we mean by relational approaches and how do these differ from more traditional behaviour management approaches?

What are relational approaches?

What do we mean by relational approaches, often also referred to as trauma-informed or attachment-aware approaches? As discussed in Chapter 2, at the very heart of these approaches is the knowledge that a feeling of connection with others and feeling of belonging are profoundly important to our wellbeing. When we feel safe and seen, we gain the capacity for growth and learning. When we feel secure and held in mind, we can face challenges, risk making mistakes, and develop our resilience. When we feel contained and heard, we can experience, understand, and regulate emotional reactions to the world, learning, and each other.

This is the broader concept of relational approaches that is connected with physical and psychological wellbeing. Under this are connections and interactions with key people, family, friends, teaching staff, and other important people in the community. Interrelated is the right environment to enable relationships to happen, the physical space, the time, the spirit, and the commitment to creating a relational world.

There do seem to be a number of barriers to effectively and consistently embedding relational approaches in schools. One potential barrier is the inconsistency in guidance developed by the Department for Education (DfE) and other organisations. These documents offer contradictory messages school staff have to grapple with. For example, the National Institute for Health and Care Excellence (NICE, 2022) guidelines for Social, Emotional and Mental Wellbeing in Primary and Secondary Schools focus on psychological safety and ensuring every school has a "culture, ethos and practice that strengthen Relational Approaches and inclusion" (NICE, 2022, 1.1.4). In contrast, while the Behaviour in Schools document (DfE, 2024) mentions calm, safe, and supportive environments, it also focuses on promoting pupil self-discipline and proper regard for authority, a duty to follow behaviour policies, and the sanctions and consequences that will occur if this does not happen. Very different messages. The pupil views work carried out by the authors of this book was used as expert testimony by NICE when updating the 2022 guidelines. We were very honoured that the pupils' views contributed to the focus on relational approaches.

Another barrier are the perceptions around what relational approaches are. There have been vocal misconceptions, with the belief that any behaviour is permitted, and this seems to have been easily taken up by the media. Contrary to what some commentators may believe, relational approaches are not and should not be without structure and purpose. What relational approaches are trying to move away from is the pure behaviourist models of consequences and "zero tolerance" behaviour management approaches, which are popular in many schools.

Another very real barrier to relational approaches is that they do take time, effort, and patience in the short term, although they save a lot in resources and time in the long term. They are not a quick fix, nor are they a one-size-fits-all intervention. Nothing is, but there seems to be a reluctance to move from the traditional tried, tested, but not universally successful, approaches. There is a long way to go to change the minds and open the hearts of some in the education sector, but if enough people take the time to try and tweak, then change can happen.

Research conducted by Jones et al. (2024) suggests that teaching staff feel Behaviourist Approaches are familiar, quick, and simple; they also offer an observable response to an event, which can be perceived as "doing something". However, the teaching staff also felt that Behaviourist Approaches created reliance on extrinsic motivations and didn't always equal long-term change. In contrast the teaching staff Jones et al. (2024) interviewed felt that relational approaches were flexible and created safety and curiosity, but they were also time-consuming (to embed and see change) and required shifts in the perceptions of staff, parents, and pupils. So relational approaches appeared to be welcomed and elements of Behaviourist Approaches were seen as helpful, but the two approaches seem to be seen as mutually exclusive.

I wonder why these two things are seen as opposed or repelling, and how difficult it seems to align these perspectives more closely. Behaviourist ideas are not all good or bad; neither are relational approaches. In fact, the more we take an integrated approach, the more we will be able to implement rich, multifaceted, and inclusive systems. This also includes acknowledging there is not going to be one "off-the-shelf" fix. Each school, trust, community, town, region, etc. has its own cultural, historical, and situational mix. However, we can, should, and will eventually find a proactive, inclusive, and flexible framework that can be adapted. There are so many examples of good practice – too many for this chapter – but we will explore some pertinent ideas below. We do need to keep exploring, sharing, and adding to our knowledge base so we can fully appreciate the power of relationships and see the impact in practice.

Relational trauma requires relational healing (Treisman, 2018)

Dr Karen Treisman (a clinical psychologist) has written comprehensively and eloquently about the importance of relationships, particularly for children and young people who have experienced unsettled or abusive early experiences (Treisman, 2016).

Research has explored the importance of early relationships on development for over 100 years. One of the most recognised concepts is Attachment Theory (Bowlby, 1969), which explores the psychological impact of early attachment relationships and the impact this can have on development. Theories around attachment suggest that children who experience consistent love and attuned relationships with their parents are more likely to thrive than children who experience inconsistent, abusive, or absent parenting (Gerhardt, 2004; Winnicott, 1971). These ideas continue to be adapted and considered, with phrases such as developmental trauma now used to conceptualise the impact of adverse early experiences.

Developmental trauma refers to the impact of early adverse experiences on a child's development. This includes their physical, emotional, social, and cognitive development. These experiences are now commonly named Adverse Childhood Experiences (ACEs), which were briefly introduced in Chapter 2. The concept of ACEs was developed by clinicians in the United States who were exploring factors that might contribute to adult health conditions, such as heart disease, alcoholism, and depression (Felitti et al., 1998). Felitti and colleagues found that individuals who had been exposed to childhood emotional, physical, or sexual abuse and household dysfunction were highly likely to have multiple health risk factors later in life.

Unfortunately, many children and young people experience adverse early experiences, in a range of ways. This includes those explored by Felitti et al. (1998) and others, such as traumatic bereavement and the types of displacement and trauma experienced by refugees. Experiences of foster care, changes in school, poverty, and social inequality also have an impact, as do factors such as racism, homophobia, and discrimination in relation to additional needs, socio-economic standing, and other factors.

These factors impact how a child develops their sense of self, their trust in others, and how they feel other people perceive them. Work by Karen Treisman (2016, 2018) and Bruce Perry (2006) allow us to understand how a lack of safety, consistency, and care in the early years can have a profound impact on a child's social and emotional development. A child may feel they need to face the world with a range of defences, which can be perceived as aggressive, antisocial, or withdrawn. Because of their mistrust of relationships, these children and young people use these defences to keep people away. Anger, high emotion, or withdrawal are responses that tend to push people away.

Why would a child trust an adult if their primary carers had not been able to provide a safe and consistent environment for that child? If all you have known is uncertainty and unsettledness, you develop your own defences and carry them with you. This is why many children and young people find school such a difficult place to navigate: so many social relationships, so much trust needed to make mistakes and learn, and so much to lose if the adult or friend lets them down. These children and young people who are in the most need of care and empathy often find this too hard to accept and so perpetuate a vicious cycle of difficult relationships. This brings us back to the quotation mentioned in our introduction: "The child who is not embraced by the village will burn it down to feel its warmth".

While there is an argument that a rule-based, authoritarian approach works for many children, the question is: how does it work? It is an approach based on fear and control, and while many will follow rules to avoid the consequences, this is not a comfortable space to be in. Indeed, in history, this has not resulted in harmony. It is another reason to explore and promote relational approaches.

Educational settings and the staff within them can offer children and young people a safe base and secondary attachment figures. They should be environments where children and young people can feel safe and know that emotionally available adults are there to support, care, and hold them in mind. This is the case for children and young people who come from safe and secure families, and it is even more vital for those who do not have this experience. This is why relational approaches work for all and should be the starting point and overall ethos in schools as they work for all. A child who comes from a settled background can still experience pressures and stress, while a child who comes from an unsettled background deserves a place of safety as a human right.

If we return to the question posed in the introduction, "what do we want our children to have learned by the time they leave school?", what were your answers? My answers were focused on kindness, acceptance, tolerance, enjoyment, being a good friend, and contributing in a positive way – qualities and values that feel joyful and should be at the centre of every setting that offers education to children and young people. These elements are central to relational approaches.

To really embed relational approaches across education, we need a consistent and clear overview of what this is, and we hope to provide some examples in the last section of this chapter. We accept and acknowledge that change is not easy, and bringing in a shift to relational approaches is no different. However, there are growing examples of where it is working; there is hope and evidence to change the hearts and minds of those who are not convinced.

How do we create change?

To create change we need to work on multiple levels. As already mentioned, there is no quick fix and there is no one-size-fits-all answer. What we will consider in this section is how we can create change at different levels and in different ways; this includes big changes and small, from top-down and bottom-up. The most important ingredient is collaboration, a core element of relationships! So let's consider these layers.

Top-down/bottom-up

A theme that comes up across the documents created to promote mental health, positive behaviour, and to safeguard children and young people in school is the need for calm, safe, respectful environments. The crucial way to create safe, calm, respectful environments is through relationships. Relationships create a sense of belonging, a feeling of trust and safety. When you are in an environment of safety, then the need for defence mechanisms and survival responses is reduced. We connect with others when we feel safe and calm; when we connect with others we learn with and from them. Learning, after all, is the primary task of the school, and relationships are at the very heart of successful learning.

So, in practical terms we need to think about how to promote relational approaches across the school for children, young people, and adults. But what does this look like?

Creating a relational ethos in educational settings

A community ethos will be the foundation for relational approaches. All educational settings have a written mission statement or set of values to show their ethos, but how is this decided and how is this embedded into the heart of the setting? This is the job of the leadership team in the school, and here we suggest two concepts to guide robust and heartfelt ways for leadership teams to develop a relational ethos and make it a reality in the day-to-day life of the community. These concepts are prosocial approaches (Atkins et al., 2019; Gillard et al., 2022) and trauma-informed approaches (Treisman, 2018; Perry, 2006). These complement the ideas around compassionate leaderships explored in Chapter 2.

Prosocial approaches

Firstly we will look at the concept of prosocial processes (Atkins et al., 2019; Gillard et al., 2022), which allows us to consider ethos from the top down with a focus on group co-operation and dynamics. There is not the space here to go into depth about this incredible framework and the thinking that underpins it, i.e. Ostrom's (1990) Nobel-winning work on Core Design Principles and Acceptance and Commitment Therapy (ACT, Hayes et al., 1999). There are references and links for you to follow to find out more, but here we will draw predominantly upon the work of Gillard et al. (2022), which focuses explicitly on prosocial approaches in schools, to provide a summary of how this may work in developing the foundation for a Relational ethos in educational settings.

Prosocial processes (Atkins et al., 2019; Gillard et al., 2022) are fundamentally about how social connectedness, cooperation, and adaptability impact on the functioning of groups (Atkins et al., 2019; Gillard et al., 2022). Atkins et al. proposed a slightly adapted version of Ostrom's eight Core Design Principles (CDPs) to understand what groups need to do in order to be cooperative and effective. For the purpose of this chapter, we will focus on the first six CDPs, as these consider, within group processes, which is more pertinent to developing a group/educational setting ethos. See Table 3.1 for an overview of these six principles, which we have adapted further to consider education settings more explicitly. We invite you to see these principles in relation to your setting and your position in it.

Prosocial processes also incorporate Acceptance and Commitment Therapy (ACT, Hayes et al., 1999) principles to support the implementation of these ideas in practical and functional ways. In summary, ACT is a therapeutic approach that aims to develop an individual's psychological flexibility, and their ability to be in the present moment, think, and commit

Table 3.1 Group dynamics

Six CDPs for cooperative group dynamics in educational settings		
1.	Shared Identity and Purpose	A shared sense of group identity and what it means to be part of this educational setting. There is a shared purpose, which is coherent and meaningful to the whole setting and the individual members.
2.	Equitable Distribution of Contributions and Benefits	It is accepted that individual members will offer different contributions to the educational settings function and purpose. There is an awareness that variation of contribution is part of effective and cooperative processes within an educational setting. The distribution of contributions and benefits are proportionate and transparent to all in the setting.
3.	Fair and Inclusive Decision-Making	The educational setting is run on principles of trust and mutually valued relationships, where individual members feel enabled and empowered to have a voice in decision-making.
4.	Monitoring Agreed Actions	To monitor and take responsibility for the fulfilment of agreed actions, functions, and purpose of the educational setting. This will include leadership overview and collective involvement in monitoring.
5.	Graduated Responses to Helpful and Unhelpful Actions	The educational setting has effective ways to respond to both helpful and unhelpful actions, which promote or impede the purpose and values of the group.
6.	Fast and Fair Conflict Resolution	An acknowledgement that conflict in group dynamics is natural, but the setting uses restorative practices that are effective, embedded, fair, and efficient.

to values-guided action. Within prosocial processes, the emphasis shifts from the individual in isolation to the dynamic of individuals interacting in a group for a common purpose, which brings us back to the CDPs mentioned above. There are a wide range of ACT processes and strategies that support prosocial processes. However, the most often used is the ACT Matrix (Gillard et al., 2022). See Figure 3.1 later in the chapter for an example of the ACT Matrix.

These concepts and processes are brought to life in the next section, where we draw on the work of Gillard et al. (2022) and our own work using these approaches with schools to inform the ways an educational setting can work together, using prosocial approaches, to achieve a relational ethos. This is outlined below.

Using prosocial approaches to develop a relational ethos

Here we will offer a constructed example (taken from a variety of ideas, conversations, and experiences) to bring the prosocial approach to life. In this example, we will focus on XY Secondary School, who wish to adapt and enhance anti-bullying policies and procedures as part of their overall relational school ethos. We have chosen anti-bullying as the focus for this example as it was an area the children and young people returned to many times in our research. For example, one child said: *"i chose other because bullying isnt on there and bullying has a negative impact on meantal health beacuse it can put you down [sic]"*.

This example also highlights how the CDPs interweave, rather than being a linear progression of actions or tasks to get to a particular outcome. It is a dynamic process.

CDP 1

XY Secondary School had decided to introduce a whole school relational approach. School-wide thinking had been done with staff and children to create a shared purpose and engagement with this approach. An initial focus was placed on agreeing the values that were felt to be important to guide thinking about relational approaches and belonging across the school. Three core values were agreed: Trust, Connectedness, and Interest/Curiosity.

This established a shared purpose to the overall focus on relational processes. The next stage was to look at particular areas for development and create working groups for these areas.

CDP 2 and 3

It was decided that different groups would be created to take on different tasks and purposes in developing the relational ethos. One of the areas of

Relationships, relationships, relationships

development was to focus on developing an anti-bullying ethos in school. This was an area the pupils identified as a concern, and they were enabled and empowered to share these views and work with staff on an issue that was relational at its core. This reinforced the CDP 1 within this smaller group as there was a coherent shared purpose.

CDP 3 and 4

To develop thinking about anti-bullying further, a working group of senior leadership staff, teaching staff, and pupils was created and different tasks given to different members of the group. One group task was to use the ACT Matrix to explore actions and feelings in relation to this anti-bullying ethos; what would it look like if the school community were moving towards anti-bullying values, and what would it be like if they were moving away from these values? An example of what an ACT Matrix exploring this area might look like is presented in Figure 3.1.

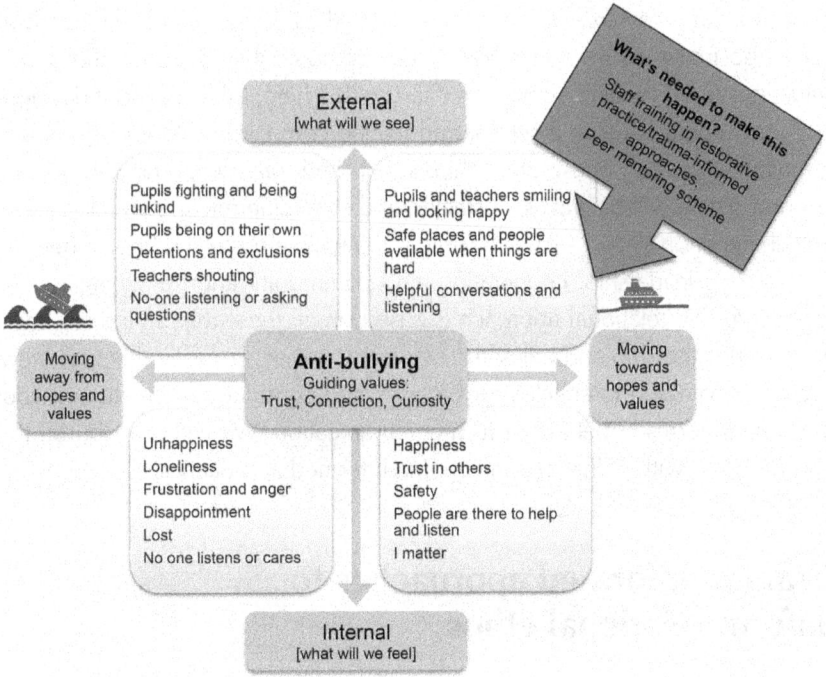

Figure 3.1 ACT Matrix

CDP 4, 5, and 6

The ACT Matrix can then be used as a guide to change, shared more widely with staff teams and pupil groups. This includes plans for training, resources, and tasks. This would then enable shared responsibility and engagement across the community, and enable collective collaboration to ensure the internal and external elements could be monitored, adapted, and supported by all involved. Collaborative decisions made early on about conflict resolution and helpful actions will create openness about the difficulties faced, and a plan will be developed with which to manage these potential difficulties.

The prosocial processes in this example are multi-layered and reflect the wider work of creating a relational school ethos and the more specific work of the group developing the anti-bullying approach. It will also be mirrored in the way the whole community interacts with each other in this relational environment because the development and the reality of living this way are bi-directional. The cooperation in the planning will permeate through its realisation as an ethos. Top-down and bottom-up.

This is a very simplistic imagining of what will be a complex and ongoing task of change towards a relational school ethos. Using approaches such as ACT also invites us to draw upon metaphors to enable ideas, emotions, and situations to be thought about. We can use that here, thinking about developing a relational ethos in a school and maybe comparing it to turning around a huge cargo ship. These huge ships need time, precision, and care to turn around. There will be waves, obstacles, and even differences of opinion about which direction to go, as it will be with shifting the ethos of a school. However, with strong leadership, cooperation, and community effort anything can be achieved. The relational approach is based on all these things, and we invite you to turn the ship and enjoy the new view. When taking in this new view, we also invite you to check your bearings and consider the direction of your thinking in terms of behaviour as a communication. We will take you on this journey now with a dive into the trauma-informed approaches.

Trauma-informed approaches to inform relational ethos

The second framework that is vital to a relational school environment is knowledge and understanding of trauma-informed approaches. Chapter 2 explored some strategies that are based on trauma-informed awareness as alternatives to reward and punishment approaches. Here we go a little deeper. We suggest the work of Beacon House (Lyons et al., 2020), Bruce Perry (2006) and Karen Treisman (2018) to guide thinking and practice. If we continue the metaphor started above, trauma-informed approaches could be the compass of the prosocial ship, giving us some direction on understanding the origins, meaning, and purpose of all behaviour, but in particular the behaviour of children and young people who have experienced trauma.

Trauma-informed approaches are a vital component to a relational ethos as it informs a belief system that is grounded in the idea of behaviour, as communication offers a relational lens with which to understand how children, young people, and adults act and react as a result of their previous experiences. This includes an awareness that behaviour manifests in physical and psychological ways. This includes a move towards understanding behaviour as communication and awareness that the actions and reactions that are often described as challenging are in fact communications of distress.

A relational ethos and approach acknowledge and appreciate that children, young people, and adults can respond to adversity in sometimes unhelpful ways. Using our compass metaphor again, children might go in different developmental directions depending on a course they were set on very young in life. A relational approach that incorporates the neurosequential model (Perry, 2006) is curious about what a behaviour is communicating and how these communications can differ due to a wide range of factors. This includes being aware that our body, our nervous system, can sometimes respond in automatic ways that have been learned through past experiences. This is a space where understanding patterns of behaviour and how they can become automatic is vital. Also vital is a need to understand factors like how a child or young person is communicating their distress, work with them to find more helpful ways for them to communicate what is happening, and then in turn build more positive relationships that will offer the stability they need.

This focuses us on behaviour as communication, alongside the acceptance that there is a biological element to our actions and with the acknowledgement that relationships can support new ways of responding. This moves us away from a pure behaviourist framework of cause, effect, and consequence; these factors are at play, but it is too one-dimensional to base a community ethos on these factors alone. Having a trauma-informed approach allows us to focus on the children and young people who need the most specific support, while also incorporating the trauma-informed organisations approach (Treisman, 2018) already discussed. These concepts combined will enable understanding and proactive and practical approaches to support all in the community, pupils, staff, and families.

This is not a quick fix, but we believe that the children and young people who have experienced trauma deserve more than a quick fix. They deserve time and care to be taken in creating an environment where they feel safe and where they belong; where they feel part of a nurturing and caring environment, but their individual needs are understood and supported. This is the top-down–bottom-up approach that we have returned to throughout this chapter: policies, ethos, and inclusion from the top down, and an understanding of individual needs from the bottom up.

In the final section of this chapter, we will briefly look at a few other important components for creating a relational school.

A relational learning environment

To continue with our ship metaphor, the different components that make up a relational ethos can be seen as the different elements that are needed to effectively run a ship. We also need to keep in mind that these elements need to be adapted, updated, and re-tuned. This includes elements such as the overall curriculum, which we will touch on below but is explored in more depth in Chapter 5, and the learning environment (for staff and pupils), which we will consider in more detail in this chapter.

A relational curriculum

A relational school ethos is augmented by a curriculum that builds relational skills. We will consider this in more depth later in the book, but it is important to ground the curriculum in the thinking we have done in this chapter about a relational ethos. This includes and goes beyond the academic content of the curriculum and acknowledges the importance of developing resilience, metacognitive skills, and emotional literacy. This leans into the concept of 21st century learning skills (Paige, 2009; Stanley-Duke and Stringer, 2017) and core work skills (World Economic Forum, 2025), which we will refer to often in this book. The World Economic Forum (WEF) has for many years outlined skills predicted to be required for future workforces to be effective, the most recent top ten skills of which are as follows.

Core skills for successful workforces (WEF, 2025)

1. Analytical thinking
2. Resilience, flexibility, and agility
3. Leadership and social influence
4. Creative thinking
5. Motivation and self-awareness
6. Technological literary
7. Empathy and active listening
8. Curiosity and life-long learning
9. Talent management
10. Service orientation and customer service

What is significant in that list is the amount of relational skills that are included. This list is compiled from employers across a wide range of industries across the world. So for a current and future workforce to be successful, relational skills are required, and these skills need to be acknowledged, developed, and celebrated in educational settings. It is interesting to note that reading, writing, and mathematics comes in at number 26! We believe the content of the curriculum is less important than the process of developing the skills needed for life, and the WEF's findings about core skills seem to support this. The thoughts children and young people shared with us also support this idea, as shown in the following quote: *"More life lessons that will help in actual life"*.

The relational curriculum includes elements like working together as a team for a mutual purpose (regardless of whether you are friends or not). It includes developing altruism and empathy, being able to give and care about others, and contribute to your community. This brings us back to the prosocial processes that we have considered as a guide to creating a relational curriculum. We create a relational ethos and we create learners who have resilience, motivation, curiosity, and the capacity for creative thinking, self-awareness, and empathy. This can be created through relationships.

A relational learning environment for all

A relational learning environment does not relate to the pupils only; it must also include the school staff as a whole, and that is what we will consider here. Including the school staff as a whole involves providing training across the school: to Senior Leadership, Teaching Assistants, the Site Manager, Office Staff, Teachers, Taxi Drivers – anyone who interacts with the children and young people in the school system should be informed of the power of relationships and the way relational approaches can create positivity. This training should not be a one-off event, but something that is explored, revisited, and adapted every day, month, term, and year. It is an ongoing process because life is an ongoing process. We should embrace relational approaches with the knowledge that it will be constantly evolving and not a quick fix, and we should meet it with curiosity and a joy for learning and development. If we have that as adults, we can model it to the children and young people.

The importance of continuous professional development (CPD) and supervision is set out in professional and ethical guidelines for Educational Psychologists. While teaching staff do need to undergo training through the school year, there is not always the emphasis on this being an embedded part of life-long learning and development. Schools have development plans for CPD across the school and individual skill development. I wonder what this CPD development might look like if it were approached with a relational lens and with prosocial processes. What would be included alongside curriculum development, and what would complement and enhance safeguarding training?

There are so many paths to go down for CPD and resources that can develop skills, which are beyond the scope of this chapter. Chapter 9 explores what next and offers some additional ideas for resources and training. To end this chapter, we do want to consider an element of staff development that is explicitly relational and we feel is fundamental to creating the relational ethos we have proposed – supervision for staff.

The relational power of supervision

Supervision as an intrinsic part of staff wellbeing was introduced in Chapter 1. We acknowledge that it is not something that usually happens as a standard practice in many schools, and often this type of support is introduced when things may not be working or there is a problem. This then leads to supervision or mentoring being seen in a negative light in education, rather than the relational space that it offers with opportunities for collaboration, reflection, and celebration. In fact, a core part of prosocial processes is reflecting on our actions, and exploring strengths and weaknesses, so we can then decide on the next action; then this cycle is repeated.

For any of the ideas posited above to work there also need to be space and time for reflection and critical analysis – "how is this going?" These spaces are needed for children, young people, and staff. This draws on a suggestion offered by a young person who responded to one of our surveys with an idea to support wellbeing: *"A wellbeing hub so that those who need it can have their own space to sit in serenity"*.

Education has so little space for reflection. I feel very honoured as an EP to spend time with teaching staff to think about what is happening for them and the children they work with. This time is not always easily found and is often felt to be something extra when needed, rather than what it should be: a monthly space to reflect and process work, relationships, and emotions; a safe space to acknowledge how difficult this work is and the energy it takes; time to be able to see the small steps of progress that can get lost in larger expectations; time to celebrate as an individual or group; a space to be honest.

I feel privileged to hear the stories and experiences of teaching staff of all levels. There is empowerment to be gained from being truly listened to and having a safe space to share and reflect in a non-judgemental and unconditional way. I have worked in this way with individuals and in groups. The groups might be from within the same school, or across different schools, brought together for the sole reason of thinking together. These sessions have always been a shared experience, with me learning as much from the people I speak to as they may learn from me. The feedback often focuses on the power of having time to think and share; on collaboration and cooperation; feeling valued and validated; reciprocal sharing of ideas and experiences – relational.

Final thoughts

Relationships are key in creating a sense of belonging and safety; this then enables a capacity to be curious, to learn and grow. When kindness and connection is experienced, it is often reciprocated. If kindness and connection is unfamiliar, then this might feel alien at first, but relationships will create a safer environment to develop trust than relationships based purely on discipline. If an environment provides the sense of feeling seen and known, this can create a motivation to learn. But more importantly, this also generates a desire to make a positive contribution to this environment and others. There may still be difficulties and differences, but the environment is a place where these things are understood, held, and celebrated.

This is the case for everyone – children, young people, and adults.

Key takeaways

1. Relational approaches can create a connected community. Children, young people, and adults thrive when they experience safe and trusting relationships.
2. Prosocial approaches can strengthen a school community. Cooperation, collaboration, and connection can create a strong and productive school environment, where everyone has a chance to feel involved and empowered. It is strength-based and promotes a sense of belonging and contribution, which in turn create stronger community bonds.
3. Everyone benefits from relational approaches. Relationships are a key aspect to wellbeing. Relationships can help address the impact of developmental trauma and past adversities. The impact of being kind, connected, and collaborative can have wide-reaching positive impacts. Relational trauma requires relational repair (Treisman, 2016).

References

Atkins, P., Wilson, D. and Hayes, S., 2019. *Prosocial: Using Evolutionary Science to Build Productive, Equitable, and Collaborative Groups*. Oakland, CA: New Harbinger Publications.

Bowlby, J., 1969. *Attachment and Loss: Volume 1. Attachment*. New York: Basic Books.

Department for Education (DfE), 2024. Behaviour in Schools: Advice for head teachers and school staff. Available at: https://assets.publishing.service.gov.uk/media/65ce3721e1bdec001a3221fe/Behaviour_in_schools_-_advice_for_headteachers_and_school_staff_Feb_2024.pdf.

Gerhardt, S. 2004. *Why Love Matters: How Affection Shapes a Baby's Brain*. East Sussex: Routledge.

Felitti, V. J., Anda, R. F., Nordenberg, D., Williamson, D. F., Spitz, A. M., Edwards, V., Koss, M. P., and Marks, J. S., 1998. Relationship of childhood abuse and household dysfunction to many of the leading causes of death in adults. The Adverse Childhood Experiences (ACE) study. *American Journal of Preventive Medicine*, 14(4), pp. 245–258. https://doi.org/10.1016/s0749-3797(98)00017-8.

Gillard, D., Jackson-Brown, F., Stanley-Duke, M., Atkins, P., Anderson, B., Balfour, E., and Cooper, P., 2022. The prosocial framework: Theory, practice and applications within schools. *Educational Psychology Research and Practice*, 8(1). https://doi.org/10.15123/uel.8v1v8.

Hayes, S.C., Strosahl, K.D., and Wilson, K.G., 1999. *Acceptance and Commitment Therapy: An Experiential Approach to Behavior Change*. New York: The Guilford Press.

Jones, R., Kreppner, J., Marsh, F., and Hartwell, B., 2024. Supporting behaviour and emotions in school: An exploration into school staff perspectives on the journey from punitive approaches to relational-based approaches. *Emotional and Behavioural Difficulties*, 29(1–2), pp. 82–98. https://doi.org/10.1080/13632752.2024.2354021.

Lyons, S., Whyte, K., Stephens, R., and Townsend, H., 2020. Developmental trauma close up. Beacon House Therapeutics and Trauma Team. Available at: https://beaconhouse.org.uk/wp-content/uploads/2020/02/Developmental-Trauma-Close-Up-Revised-Jan-2020.pdf.

National Institute for Health and Care Excellence (NICE), 2022. Social, emotional and mental wellbeing in primary and secondary education. NG223. Available at: https://www.nice.org.uk/guidance/ng223.

Ostrom, E., 1990. *Governing the Commons: The Evolution of Institutions for Collective Action*. Cambridge: Cambridge University Press. https://doi.org/10.1017/CBO9781316423936.

Paige, J., 2009. The 21st century skills movement. *Educational Leadership*, 9(67), p. 11.

Perry, B.D., 2006. Applying principles of neurodevelopment to clinical work with maltreated and traumatized children: The neurosequential model of therapeutics. In N.B. Webb (Ed.), *Working with Traumatized Youth in Child Welfare* (pp. 27–52). New York: The Guilford Press.

Popoola, M. and Sivers, S., 2021. Hearing the voices of children and young people: An ecological systems analysis of individual difference and experiences during the Covid-19 lockdown. *DECP Debate*, 177, pp. 21–25.

Popoola, M. and Sivers, S., 2023. Maslow, relationships and square pegs. In F. Morgan and E. Costello (Eds.), *Square Pegs: Inclusivity, Compassion and Fitting In: A Guide for Schools* (pp. 77–88). Bancyfelin: Independent Thinking Press.

Sivers, S., Wendland, S., Baggley, L., and Boyle, K., 2022. What children and young people told us as the Covid-19 pandemic unfolded. In C. Arnold and B. Davis (Eds.), *Children in Lockdown: Learning the Lessons of Pandemic Times*. London: Karnac.

Stanley-Duke, M. and Stringer, P., 2017. What is the meaning of "employability" and how can educational psychologists' involvement at post-16 embrace it? *DECP Debate*, 164, pp. 9–16.

Treisman, K., 2016. *Working with Relational and Developmental Trauma in Children and Adolescents*. London: Routledge.

Treisman, K., 2018. *Becoming a More Culturally, Adversity, and Trauma-Informed, Infused, and Responsive Organisation*. London: Winston Churchill Fellowship Report.

Winnicott, D.W., 1971. *Playing and Reality*. London: Penguin.

World Economic Forum (WEF), 2025. *Future of Jobs Report 2025: Insight Report*. Geneva: World Economic Forum.

4

What will it take to create a genuine meaning of the term "mentally healthy schools"?

Maddi Popoola

> *Mental health needs to be as important as grades.*
> Child

> *School has a negative impact as many teachers put a lot of pressure onto people my age and it can be too much to handle sometimes. I start to panic when I need to remember lots of stuff.*
> Child

What is the problem?

Whether you work in the world of children's mental health or you just have a social media account, it is hard to avoid statistics that are being postulated around the decline of our children's mental health. The Children's Society, renowned for the data reports and statistics they produce, released the Good Childhood Report in 2022, which outlines that, in the previous three years, the likelihood of children having a mental health problem has increased by 50% and, furthermore, an estimated 5 children in every classroom of 30 are likely to have a mental health "problem" (Children's Society, 2022).

When we talk about mental health, it is important to define what we mean and to reflect on the remaining negative connotations this term brings to mind for some, often linked to negative presentations such as "anxiety", "low mood", and "depression". Yet, mental health, as defined by the World Health Organization (WHO, 2022), is "a state of mental well-being that enables people to cope with the stresses of life, realize their abilities, learn well and work well, and contribute to their community". The opposition to this is what we may consider to be mental disorder or a mental health difficulty.

It is important to acknowledge the non-linear human experience of mental health or mental difficulty and the ongoing interactions between a human and their environmental experiences that impact on both health and difficulty, linked to many other factors of resilience, social support, and other life experiences that interact with our feelings and state of mind. A mental health disorder is a condition that affects your mood, thinking, and behaviour. This may happen over a short period of time or come and go, and some can be chronic (long-lasting). They can affect your ability to relate to others and function each day. This is important when we are defining and thinking about what mental health means, particularly when defining and envisaging a mentally healthy school, because the focus of this is to support each and every individual to feel good, and function well, rather than what may be linked to more targeted support for mental disorder or mental ill health. Support for this is of course important, but not what constitutes the foundations of a mentally healthy school.

Given the claimed statistics around the decline of children's mental health, it is surely essential that, in order to understand the problem, we have to look into and consider the *why*. One way of exploring this is to start to develop an understanding of the world of children living through the modern world: what is it like to be a child in 2024? What are the factors contributing to mental health in both positive and negative ways? How do children make sense of their life experiences, and how do these things impact on their mental health?

In 2023, Popoola and Sivers, as part of the ongoing "pupil views" work referenced in this book, set out to answer the above questions through a survey asking young people about their mental health: 640 children from UK school year groups 5 through to 13 responded to the survey and the full findings can be read in our full report published online (Popoola and Sivers, 2023). The key learnings from the survey form the basis of this chapter and the foundations to consider the impact of school on mental health and mental disorder.

What do children say is the problem?

Firstly, 63% of the children who responded to our survey felt they were coping with life either most or some of the time. This left the stark figure of 37% finding it difficult to cope some or most of the time. While this is a worrying figure, it is important to acknowledge that increased awareness of negative terms linked to mental health will account for some of this reporting, because new initiatives to raise the profile will inevitably lead to increased acknowledgement and self-awareness.

The next question gave a range of options for children to answer on the things they feel have a positive impact on their mental health. They were able to select more than one answer and also select "other". They were then asked to elaborate on answers with a qualitative narrative. Results were, unsurprisingly, overwhelmingly linked to relationships and human connection: 71% of children identified friends as having a positive impact on their mental health, and 74% identified their family; 26% of children said school and 27% felt social media has a positive impact on their mental health. The "other" category was selected by 28% of respondents, and the qualitative analysis uncovered a range of suggestions linked to the activities in life that we would consider to contribute to those key feelings of happiness and functioning, such as the arts, physical activity, nature, hobbies, food, and religion.

Themes of psychological needs were threaded through the views shared with us, which provided further insights into the way each factor (family, friends, school/college, and social media) had a positive influence on mental health. Family and friends were more likely to offer opportunities for relatedness, emotional wellbeing, and psychological safety. School/college was more likely to improve mental health through opportunities for learning and growth. Social media was more likely than any other group to offer opportunities for distraction from mental health issues.

In contrast, we asked children to identify from the same list what they felt was having a negative impact on their mental health, and again the option to select "other" was presented, followed by a question to gain an understanding of *why* children selected answers through qualitative narrative. Results told us that, overall, the highest number and percentage of young people identified school as having a negative impact on their mental health. Over 50% of respondents selected "school" when answering the question. This is proportionally higher than the number of young people who selected any of the remaining categories (friendships 19%, family 13%, social media 36%, and "other" 36%).

The qualitative responses gave us a more in-depth understanding of why school is a key contributor to poor mental health. One key quote that I use repeatedly in presenting this work to schools and other agencies stands out as a narrative that gets to the heart of the matter:

> *I feel like my grades define me as a person as the teachers constantly remind us they expect all of us to get 9s and grades that are better than average, which makes so many of us average students feel like we're disappointing them. I'm more worried about my teachers reactions [sic] to my GCSEs than what my actual grades will be. I'm burnt out. I haven't been able to do homework in a little over a year because of these expectations that haven't made me want to do well, but just make me want GCSEs over and done with. I'm not even scared or stressed about them anymore, which is pretty scary itself to be honest, because it's a daily threat that's been used so much it doesn't even seem to mean anything anymore.*
>
> Child

Expectations, disappointment, worry, burn out, scary, threat – words that we found repeatedly used in relation to school. The word "stress" alone was counted 66 times in the qualitative data and four key themes were identified:

- **Stress and worry:** *"I have been given a lot of stress and pressure because of school, plus there are high expectations that I barely manage to meet".*
- **Fear and rules:** *"School rules are strict. I lose time learning which is supposed to be the most important thing for something stupid like talking in line."*
- **Relationships (poor relationships and bullying):** *"I was bullied at school and they did nothing to really resolve the issue. I also struggled with the school environment but again school were unsupportive. This in turn affected my physical health too."*
- **Homework and exams as a key source of pressure:** *"School makes me worry about handing in homework on time and staying up late so I can do it school can really stress me out, it can overload me with lots of homework etc.".*

It is important to be careful here that blame is not pointed towards school staff who work tirelessly to support children in school with their academic and pastoral needs. What is coming through here in the data is a greater problem of systemic pressure that is flooding into every aspect of school life and all those working within it. Headteachers and SLTs (senior leadership teams) are under pressure to produce results through positive Progress 8 scores, SAT results, phonics screenings, and of course the "dreaded Ofsted" inspections. At the time of writing this, the new government have recently released new legislation around inspections to scrap the Ofsted grades, and conversations about school success being measured by inclusion are becoming more fruitful. But there is a long way to go to turn the tides meaningfully so that our children are not the victims of the wider systemic pressures that currently impact on wellbeing.

I am not sure how we have arrived at a place in which strict school rules based on outdated behaviourist systems, pressure for academic success, and a lack of focus on relationships has become the norm within education. I have read theories around the need for compliance as a key component in the way our education system was set up when it was in its infancy, to ensure we have a compliant workforce, a non-questioning society to enable leaders to impose what they will upon us without question, to ensure the workforce is compliant and "hardworking". I am not sure these values ever did underpin the basis of the education system, but if they did, surely it's now time to move on?

I recently met with a young person in year 8 at secondary school. She was referred into mental health services and was receiving support from CAMHS (Child and Adolescent Mental Health Services). She was engaging in regular "self-harming behaviours" in school, not attending lessons but attending school daily, and she was described by school staff as being their biggest current challenge in terms of understanding needs, behaviours, and how to manage her.

I met with her in a room in the school inclusion area, and she asked that her mum not join us. Her opening words to me reminded me of my own 13-year-old: *"miss I ain't gonna cry ya know, i'm a big man [sic]".*

She was right, and for the first 45 minutes, she proceeded to talk, shouting in parts, very expressively. I enjoyed my time speaking to her as she was open and honest. Towards the end of the session, I asked her how she felt about school and the people there. She told me how much she liked it: *"Mr x, he's like my dad, they are my family here".*

What a wonderful thing to hear, and I made a mental note to reflect to the staff working with her how special it is that she feels connected to them. I don't doubt most children in schools feel this towards the adults who work so tirelessly every day to support children through the hardest years of their life (i.e. the teenage years!).

Something then happened: she started to become tearful, and although my motherly instincts often make me want to reach out and give physical comfort to any child I see crying, I refrained, took a moment, and asked why speaking about school had made her feel so sad? *"Because I will get excluded, they keep reducing my time, and telling me if I don't do better they will kick me out."*

In the moment I led the conversation back with another question: *"What would that mean to you for them to kick you out?"*

"I don't know", she said, *"but they will do, even my mum keeps saying it, they don't really want me here".*

"When you harm yourself in school, is that because you feel like you've done something so wrong that they might kick you out?"

"No, not really, but I know that if I do that they feel more sorry for me and probably will send me home rather than exclude me."

The gravity of these words didn't hit me until I was driving home that day (a time when workday thoughts often collate and unjumble themselves): the threat of exclusion causing anxiety, the anxiety causing the behaviour, the behaviour causing the threat. The loop was clear – this child loved the school family she was part of, but the institutional sanction system was impacting on their actions, their language, and, subsequently, the child's mental health. I thought about a statement that I have read before that has always stood out to me and influenced both my practice as a psychologist and my parenting:

"Anxiety statements breed anxiety": *"If you don't pass your GSCEs then . . .",* and *"If you don't start to behave then . . .".*

Yes, I thought, language used to instil fear and anxiety will increase fear and anxiety, and a child on the verge of exclusion will feel pain and rejection, when all she wants to feel is that she belongs.

Current government and school solutions to creating and supporting "mentally healthy schools"

All schools should, by now, have a role within their senior leadership team (or someone supported by the SLT) who is a designated senior mental health lead for the school. This role and the implications, strengths, and limitations of it were explored in Chapter 1. This initiative was part of the Department for Education (DfE) green paper, published in 2017. The green paper set out a plan for the transformation of children's mental health services. As an Educational Psychologist working in Nottingham City in 2019, I can remember the excitement when the new "Education Mental Health Practitioner" (EMHP) roles were created and we were briefed on how this would look for our schools. Working in a local authority that had a targeted CAMHS team, our MHST (Mental Health Support Team) would sit alongside this, an unusual model for a health service, and unique in the way that it enables joint working, which was certainly an advantage for the MHST. The three core functions of the team were:

1. Working one on one and with small groups of children and young people in schools at the early intervention level, using low-intensity cognitive behavioural therapeutic techniques.
2. Delivering psychoeducation workshops, assemblies, and groups as part of the whole school approach to mental health, supporting schools to embed good practice, as outlined by the DfE, in creating mentally healthy schools (DfE, 2017).
3. Signposting schools, Senior Mental Health Leads (SMHLs), and parents to other services if MHST is not the appropriate services for that child.

The Covid-19 pandemic delayed the rollout of MHSTs in schools, not necessarily in terms of delaying any funding coming through, but certainly in operational models being developed, as the closure of schools meant a delay in practitioners embedding themselves in schools, developing relationships, and of course seeing children face to face. The latest figures set out by the DfE indicate MHSTs are now covering 54% of the school population, meaning that more than half of children should have an EMHP working in, and as part of, their school for a day per week, implementing the three core functions of the service as set out above. An EMHP working in an MHST service has a "patch" of schools in a locality, usually no more than five schools per practitioner, allowing for a model of a day per week in each school. This of course is flexible dependent on need and size of settings.

A further part of this initiative is the grant-funded offer of training for SMHLs. Several approved providers have developed training for SMHLs, who can access the training *and* access DfE funding to pay for a place on the training. The training provides delegates with a process for auditing and improving provision for mental health in schools, based on key areas, as set out by the DfE: eight principles to promoting a whole school or college approach to mental health:

1. Leadership and management
2. Ethos and environment
3. Curriculum (teaching and learning)
4. Enabling student voice
5. Staff development
6. Identifying need and monitoring impact
7. Working with parents and carers
8. Targeted support

From the eight principles above, schools are encouraged to complete an audit of their current practice in each area, showcasing what they are doing well and also highlighting gaps that can then be prioritised for change and development.

Being the service manager for an MHST, my advocacy for the service and the work they are doing to support schools is, of course, immensely biased. The green paper, the acknowledgement of the need for SMHLs in schools, and the funding provided for the rollout of MHSTs were all exceptional moves forward, and remain brilliant initiatives that will have long-lasting impact. The most recent data indicates MHSTs now account for at least 15% of the interventions for children's mental health across the UK, and this will continue to grow as more MHSTs are rolled out across the UK.

School audits using the eight principles

The principles provide a guide for schools to consider how they are promoting mental health and wellbeing across their organisation. Each principle then needs to be considered in depth, with key questions to ask and examples of implementation to be sought. Leadership and management are purposefully at the centre or "core" of the principles, because without a leadership team prioritising mental health and wellbeing for all, other principles become difficult to embed. With this in mind, I have listed key starter questions within each principle below, and would advise any school leadership team to use this as a starting point for examining and reflecting upon their current position. The questions can form the basis of an audit and be used to examine examples of practice. Where such examples are lacking, a starting point would be to reflect on why, and what can be done to change that.

Ask yourselves:
Leadership and management:

- **What are the systems in place to support the mental health and wellbeing for all (children, staff, parents)?** This needs to be considered at the organisational and individual level. Mapping this out is a good starting place!

For example:

1. Does the school have a system for staff supervision (reflective supervision rather than line management)?
2. Does the school have a child and staff wellbeing policy?
3. Do leaders place staff wellbeing at the heart of all decision-making?
4. Does the school embody and promote a community of support through school events and engagement strategies for working with parents/carers and families?
5. Do leaders promote and allow autonomy for staff in their working day and teaching practice?
6. Does the school have mental health support for children through a counselling service/MHST?
7. Do all staff have a good understanding of the local offer for children's mental health? And is this promoted to families?
8. Does the school have a service for staff mental health support where needed?
9. Does the school have a system for providing psychoeducation for children?
10. Does the school have a system for supporting staff who have been off work due to poor mental health?

Ethos and environment:

- **How does the ethos and environment in school promote respect and value diversity?**

For example:

1. Does the school meet the basic needs of children and young people, especially the most vulnerable?
2. Does the school have quiet, safe spaces for pupils who wish to retreat from busy school life? Are these spaces co-produced with students?
3. Does everyone help with cleaning up and organising communal areas in the school, e.g. playground, corridors?
4. Does the school lead activities to help the local community?
5. How does the school value, celebrate, and promote diversity?
6. How does the school include minority voices?
7. Does the school protect staff, young people, and families from discrimination?
8. How do adults speak to and about children/parents/carers in school?
9. How does the school foster and support aspirations for all students, no matter what their individual circumstances are? How are students and staff inspired?
10. How are all members of the school supported to cope with the challenges of life, e.g. access to activities, support to help others (volunteering, etc.), enrichment, emotional literacy?

Curriculum teaching and learning:

- **How is the curriculum used to promote resilience and support social and emotional learning?**

For example:

1. Does the school/college follow a recognised RSE/PSHE curriculum? Is this differentiated for young people with special educational needs and disabilities (SEND)?
2. Is mental health, social and emotional learning, and resilience embedded within all areas of the curriculum? How does each subject facilitate conversations around wellbeing?
3. How do the daily routines of school support young people's resilience and social and emotional learning? Or the opposite?
4. Are staff, young people, and parents/carers involved in curriculum teaching and learning planning, evaluation, and development?

Student voice:

- **How are students supported and enabled to influence decision-making in the school in a meaningful way?**

For example:

1. Is the voice of every learner heard and valued, and do they influence decision-making?
2. How often do leaders gather student voice, and how?
3. How do leaders act on student voice and how do they give feedback?
4. Do students feel listened to and included in significant organisational decisions?
5. Are specific events and mechanisms in place to promote student voice?
6. Are the voices and ideas of students embedded in practice?
7. Do the SLT systems clearly link with student voice and does this impact on school improvement strategy?
8. Are systems in place to gain students' feedback on their mental health needs and support available in school?

Staff development:

- **How are staff supported to manage their own wellbeing and that of students?**

For example:

1. Is staff wellbeing prioritised by SLT within all school structures?
2. Do leaders actively promote self-management and wellbeing strategies?
3. Is there regular access to support and reflective supervision (also highlighted in the leadership framework above)?
4. Are wellbeing check-ins embedded in staff appraisal?
5. Do all staff feel confident to support their own mental wellbeing, and that of pupils and students?
6. Are staff training and ongoing support provided within the continuous professional development (CPD) programme?
7. Are there specific opportunities to develop pastoral skills and mental health understanding?

8. Does your school have a staff wellbeing policy/charter/statement?
9. Is the review of mental health practice and innovations seen within all aspects of the school day and built into team development?

Identifying need and monitoring support:

- **How are the mental health needs of a child identified, and how do we monitor any interventions?**

For example:

1. Is mental health information displayed and highlighted around school? Is it visible and does it include information about relevant local services, and psychoeducation?
2. Is your SMHL in post and are they supported with additional time to do the role?
3. Does your school have an early intervention strategy to support emotional wellbeing at a targeted level, e.g. access to an ELSA.
4. Does your school have a system for identification and referral for concerns about mental health and wellbeing?
5. Does your school have access to an MHST and is your education mental health practitioner supporting to embed the "whole school approach" work such as assemblies and workshops?
6. Does your school have a data system to monitor and evaluate the impact of internal mental health referrals and interventions?

Targeted support and appropriate external referrals:

- **How does your school ensure children and young people get timely and appropriate support?**

For example:

1. Are there established relationships with a range of key individuals within different agencies who the SMHL liaises with regularly to access mental health support for children and young people?
2. Is the school/college aware of, and does it access the local educational, health, and social care systems to support mental health?

3. Does school/college involve a range of agencies and engage with mental health forums at a senior management level to shape service provision?
4. Does the school have a counselling service or school counsellor who is employed by the school?
5. Does the school facilitate access to external agencies with staff availability and space in school where needed?

Working with parents, carers, and families:

- **How are parents and carers involved in school wellbeing, and how is parent wellbeing supported?**

For example:

1. Are opportunities for collaborations identified and developed via community links?
2. Are parents/carers aware of who and how to contact someone at school in the event of a concern regarding a student? Is this support accessible to all?
3. Is information on mental health advice and help available, and how is this supported within school to be available and accessible to all?
4. How is a culture of community fostered through events and accessibility, e.g. coffee mornings and parents' evenings?
5. Does the school support local mental health services to offer work with parents, through engagement with services such as MHSTs where available?
6. Is parental mental health considered within safeguarding, and are appropriate referrals made when concerns are raised?
7. Do parents have a clear understanding of who to speak to in school if they have a concern about their child's mental health?

What else needs to change to create mentally healthy school environments?

In order to think about change, and what is needed to truly make a mentally healthy school environment, we have to start with the system itself and consider factors that may be acting against this goal. In my view, and heavily based on the ongoing feedback from children about their school experience, there are two key factors we have to do consider in more detail:

1. Relationships
2. Belonging

Relationships

When children talk about the things that contribute positively to their well-being, they usually include their friendships and relationships with teachers, where positive. Having a person to talk to and "tell", particularly when we are needing to share something linked to our mental health, is a key factor is resilience and healing. The example of "psychological partners" introduced in the England football team is a primary example of how human connection can work. Likewise, research consistently tells us that the number one factor in healing following disastrous and traumatic life events is social support. There is a reason that our answer to mental health difficulties is talking therapies, because the healing of human connection is inbuilt within us all; through our existence from conception to death, we are wired to relate and to be related to.

Relationships in schools are layered; we have relationships at an organisational level, between "management" or SLTs and the staff teams, between SLT and the students, and furthermore with the parent community and outside agencies, etc. Relationships between adults and staff are just as impactful as relationships with students; if staff relationships are good, healthy (predominantly), and respectful, staff wellbeing is much more likely to be high. Relationships between students is a further layer: how are children demonstrating compassion and kindness to each other? Children learn about relationships from their primary caregiver in their infancy, and this expands as they become older, certainly towards those who teach them. The demonstration of kindness and compassion is surely, therefore, of the utmost importance for adults in schools: treat others how we want to be treated, right?

Relationships between SLT and the organisation

A good leadership team will place relationships at the heart of school success and recognise the value of healthy relationships in underpinning achievement. It is something that seems so simple but can be extremely difficult to continually maintain and manage, not to mention exhausting. *But* the work and time saved when we get this right, and the impact on wellbeing, are worth their weight in gold. Conceptualising the mechanisms of healthy relationships is not an easy task. We can see and feel what this looks like, in the behaviour of people within the organisation and the feelings they report to have about being there, but the underpinning psychological and behavioural

"Mentally healthy schools"

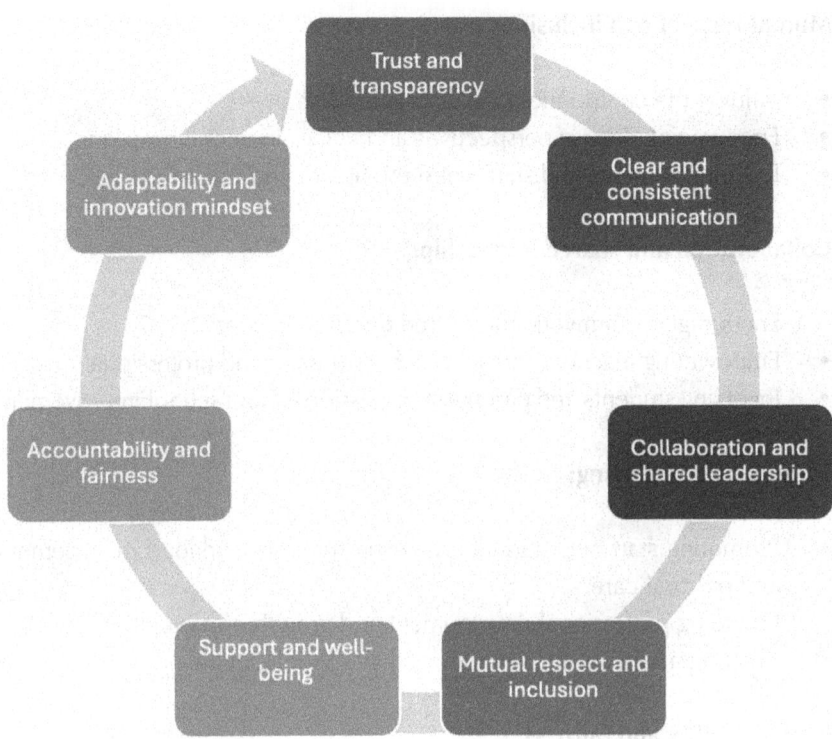

Figure 4.1 Principles for leadership

mechanisms that contribute are built on some key principles that can be used as a reflection tool for leaderships teams, summarised in Figure 4.1.

Trust and transparency:

- Open and honest communication about decisions, policies, and expectations
- A culture where feedback is valued and acted upon
- Leaders who are approachable and demonstrate integrity

Clear and consistent communication:

- Regular updates through meetings, emails, newsletters, and open-door policies
- Active listening to concerns and responding with empathy
- Clarity in vision, expectations, and responsibilities

Mutual respect and inclusion:

- Valuing the contributions of all stakeholders
- Encouraging diverse perspectives and voices in decision-making
- Ensuring students and staff feel seen, heard, and valued

Collaboration and shared leadership:

- Encouraging teamwork and shared decision-making
- Empowering teachers and staff with autonomy and professional trust
- Involving students and parents in discussions about school improvement

Support and wellbeing:

- Promoting staff and student wellbeing through workload management and pastoral care
- Providing professional development and growth opportunities
- Creating a safe, nurturing, and positive school culture

Accountability and fairness:

- Holding all members of the school community to high but fair standards
- Addressing conflicts and issues consistently and equitably
- Modelling ethical behaviour and professional standards

Adaptability and a growth (and innovative) mindset:

- Being open to feedback and willing to make changes
- Encouraging innovation and continuous improvement
- Supporting resilience and problem-solving at all levels

Relationships between staff and students

When children talk about positive aspects of their school experience, they usually include positive relationships with teachers as being a motivating and protective factor. Pupil views research into factors influencing mental health provides several examples of how children experience relationships with teachers as being helping and supportive (Popoola and Sivers, 2023):

- *"Because they encourage me to be who I am, and to feel free to open up to anyone when I feel like I need any help."*
- *"My teacher helps me in lessons."*

In contrast, when relationships with teachers are poor, children report feeling the opposite:

- *"Because teachers are so rude, [they] can sometimes make you feel angry if you're already annoyed."*
- *"Teachers are obsessed with uniform and GCSEs."*
- *"Some of the teachers are not as good with stuff and always giving c1/2 and 3s and it angers me and my mental health."*
- *"The teachers are scary, always stressed and shouting."*
- *"The teachers always shout at me for no reason."*
- *"Teachers might be able to teach, but if you want to work with kids then you need to understand them and how to work with them and they don't."*

If we can conclude that staff–student relationships are an essential contributor to wellbeing and positive mental health, it is essential that the school ethos of relationships is underpinned by mutual respect. The power balance is a component that is difficult to perfect, particularly within secondary education in the UK, and has become a fatal contributor to failing relationships. The enforcement of rules through direct and unforgiving language and the issuance of consequences school staff feel the pressure themselves to adopt, just so they can remain "in control", are detrimental. The way children are spoken to is set by senior leaders in schools, some still choosing to control through raising voices, corridor crowd control administered by the loudest and deepest of voices, alongside "tuck your shirt in", "WRONG WAY!", "WHY are you not in class", etc. The school gate is an insightful moment in time to judge what relationships are like in a school; how are your children being welcomed into school in the morning by staff? How are they spoken to? What tone is used? Do they feel persecuted before they even arrive in the building?

As a school leader, what do you know about relationships between staff and children in your school? Some questions to explore are:

- Do staff feel empowered and trusted to build relationships with children?
- Does every child have an adult in school they feel they can trust?
- How are your school systems set up to foster positive relationships (how are rules enforced with reason and kindness)?
- How much time do your students get with key adults (tutors/mentors/pastoral team/SEND team)?
- Do people in your school show genuine positive regard for each other?

Relationships between the school and community

Parental mental health is a vital component of family wellbeing, directly impacting children's academic success, emotional development, and overall behaviour. Schools are uniquely positioned to support parents in maintaining good mental health. Many parents with mental health problems are able to give their children safe and loving care, without their children being negatively affected in any way. But sometimes parents with mental health problems need support from family members, friends, neighbours, and/or professionals, to help them care for their children. Schools are often a central hub of the community, making them ideal to offer resources and support to parents. If parents feel they can come to the school for support, schools are much more likely to be successful in helping them, and hence their children. This is particularly true when working with families who have children finding it difficult to attend school, which will be discussed further in Chapter 6.

Schools are becoming places of access for children and their families, and access to all services are often through the school. Schools are now expected to make such referrals and liaise with a wide number of services and professionals in order to coordinate support. Being a member of staff in a school is no longer solely about being a teacher, due to the high social needs and daily challenges of working with children and families; schools are having to adapt to become the "front line" of care. A key component of being successful at community support is building relationships with parents and carers. This is the responsibility of each individual member of staff, to maintain contact, ensure parents are well informed, and communication is compassionate. Staff need to be trained in being trauma-informed in their understanding and responses to the community being served as well as the students, and the school itself should be an open and welcoming place for parents and outside agencies to attend.

Belonging

The introductory chapter set out the importance of belonging in relation to school: "To truly belong is to be accepted, just as you are, no matter how much you may get it wrong, or not do, or be the same as other group members".

Belonging in school is important because it is linked strongly in research to other factors, such as engagement, resilience, and higher achievement (Organisation for Economic Co-operation and Development, 2018). We are wired to belong to social groups, based on evolutionary survival (those who belonged to groups would survive longer). Defence and hunting was much easier for our ancestors who were part of a pack, and lives depended upon the protection of the group. While not so dramatic, this instinct for humans remains connected to our being, and we are more successful when we feel accepted, connected, and cared for. If you are a school leader and you want better outcomes (all outcomes, including academic), you will be interested to understand how you can ensure all members of your organisation belong.

How does a school ensure everyone belongs?

Fostering school belonging is not just about making students feel welcome – it is a foundational aspect of academic success, emotional wellbeing, and long-term resilience. By building strong relationships, promoting inclusivity, and creating a supportive environment, schools can cultivate a culture where all students feel valued and connected. Here are some key ideas:

Teacher–student relationships

- **Show genuine care and interest:** personalized greetings, knowing students' names, and acknowledging their experiences increase connectedness (Cornelius-White, 2007).
- **Provide emotional support:** teachers who actively listen and validate students' feelings create a safe space (Hughes et al., 2012).

- **Encourage student voice:** involving students in decision-making fosters agency and a sense of being valued (Juvonen et al., 2019).

Positive peer relationships

- **Cooperative learning:** group work and peer mentoring build social connections (Johnson and Johnson, 2009).
- **Inclusive social norms:** schools should implement anti-bullying programmes and promote kindness initiatives (Swearer et al., 2010).

Culturally responsive practices

- **Diverse representation in curriculum:** when students see their backgrounds reflected in materials, they feel acknowledged (Gay, 2018).
- **Identity-affirming practices:** schools should celebrate different cultures, languages, and histories to validate students' identities (Ladson-Billings, 1995).

Creating a supportive school climate

- **Welcoming environments:** visually inclusive signage, student artwork, and community-building events foster connection (Thapa et al., 2013).
- **Restorative practices:** encouraging dialogue and conflict resolution strengthens trust and mutual respect (Gregory et al., 2016).

Extracurricular engagement

- **Encourage participation:** clubs, sports, and creative activities provide social bonding opportunities (Eccles and Barber, 1999).
- **Mentoring programmes:** connecting students with older peers or teachers enhances support networks (Rhodes, 2004).

Final thoughts

School rules are a key factor in belonging. As social beings, we are far more likely to follow rules when we see purpose, because the rule is set for the greater good. Furthermore, we are more likely to follow rules if we are asked to do so, rather than told. Social conditioning and behaviourist psychology is the current pedagogy underpinning school behaviour management systems. There is very little room in the rules for mistakes to be made without punishment. Furthermore, as Paul Dix (*When the Adults Change, Everything Changes*) correctly highlights, safety for children and a sense of justice/behaviour adaptation is not instilled through fear of getting it wrong and tough consequences. This can only be taught to children by the way we teach them, the way we speak to them, and the consistency of language and care. A true human motivation to change cannot be cultivated through repeated punishment; only when the child feels they belong, they are connected, cared for, and supported can real change and learning occur. This is particularly true for our adolescents whose brains are wired for the few essential years of high-stakes schooling, to take risks, break the rules, be out of control of their emotions, rationality, decision-making, etc. You will sense my tone of failure to understand, when we have come so far in understanding brain development for children, why we maintain a system of outdated practice within education, particularly when it comes to behaviour management. Belonging and relationships need to be the fundamental underpinnings of behaviour policies if we are to truly build mentally healthy schools (Dix, 2017).

Key takeaways

1. School as both a cause and solution for mental health issues: over 50% of children surveyed identified school as having a negative impact on their mental health, mainly due to systemic pressures, strict behaviour policies, and high academic expectations (Popoola and Sivers, 2023; Children's Society, 2022). However, positive relationships with teachers were consistently reported as the most protective factor for student wellbeing.
2. Importance of relationships and belonging: the chapter emphasises that strong, supportive relationships between students and teachers, staff and leadership, and schools and parents are essential to creating a mentally healthy school culture. These relationships foster resilience, engagement, and a sense of belonging (Cornelius-White, 2007; Popoola and Sivers, 2023; Gregory et al., 2016).

3. Whole school approach through leadership and systemic change: the chapter outlines the Department for Education's (DfE, 2017) eight principles for promoting mental health in schools. These include leadership, staff development, student voice, supportive environments, and collaborative work with external agencies. The Mental Health Support Teams (MHST) model is presented as a promising intervention to embed early support and systemic change across UK schools.

References

Children's Society, 2022. The Good Childhood Report 2022. Available at: https://www.childrenssociety.org.uk/information/professionals/resources/the-good-childhood-report .

Cornelius-White, J.H.D., 2007. Learner-centered teacher-student relationships are effective: A meta-analysis. *Review of Educational Research*, 77(1), pp. 113–143.

Department for Education (DfE), 2017. Transforming Children and Young People's Mental Health Provision: A green paper. Available at: https://assets.publishing.service.gov.uk/media/5a823518e5274a2e87dc1b56/Transforming_children_and_young_people_s_mental_health_provision.pdf.

Dix, P., 2017. *When the Adults Change, Everything Changes: Seismic Shifts in School Behaviour*. Carmarthen: Crown House Publishing.

Eccles, J.S. and Barber, B.L., 1999. Student council, volunteering, basketball, or marching band: What kind of extracurricular involvement matters? *Journal of Adolescent Research*, 14(1), pp. 10–43.

Gay, G., 2018. *Culturally Responsive Teaching: Theory, Research, And Practice*. 3rd ed. New York: Teachers College Press.

Gregory, A., Clawson, K., Davis, A., and Gerewitz, J., 2016. The promise of restorative practices to transform teacher-student relationships and achieve equity in school discipline. *Journal of Educational and Psychological Consultation*, 26(4), pp. 325–353.

Hughes, J.N., Luo, W., Kwok, O., and Loyd, L.K., 2012. Teacher–student support, effortful engagement, and achievement: A 3-year longitudinal study. *Journal of Educational Psychology*, 104(3), pp. 821–835.

Johnson, D.W. and Johnson, R.T., 2009. An educational psychology success story: Social interdependence theory and cooperative learning. *Educational Researcher*, 38(5), pp. 365–379.

Juvonen, J., Espinoza, G., and Knifsend, C., 2019. The role of peer relationships in student academic and extracurricular engagement. *Educational Psychologist*, 54(4), pp. 250–264.

Ladson-Billings, G., 1995. Toward a theory of culturally relevant pedagogy. *American Educational Research Journal*, 32(3), pp. 465–491.

Organisation for Economic Co-operation and Development (OECD), 2018. *The Framework for Policy Action on Inclusive Growth*. Paris: OECD.

Popoola, M. and Sivers, S., 2023. Pupil Views Mental Health Survey Report. Available at: https://drive.google.com/file/d/1vdxravNG6MVNzhD_M3b4GMbJjRIvwWCZ/view?usp=share_link

Rhodes, J.E., 2004. The critical ingredient: Caring youth–staff relationships in after-school settings. *New Directions for Youth Development*, 2004(101), pp. 145–161.

Swearer, S.M., Espelage, D.L., Vaillancourt, T., and Hymel, S., 2010. What can be done about school bullying? Linking research to educational practice. *Educational Researcher*, 39(1), pp. 38–47.

Thapa, A., Cohen, J., Guffey, S., and Higgins-D'Alessandro, A., 2013. A review of school climate research. *Review of Educational Research*, 83(3), pp. 357–385.

World Health Organization (WHO), 2022. Mental health: Strengthening our response. Available at: https://www.who.int/news-room/fact-sheets/detail/mental-health-strengthening-our-response.

5

Academic pressure through the eyes of children
What do they really want to learn?
Maddi Popoola

I don't like exams and find it hard to show all I know in them. I'm dyslexic and it doesn't enable me to show my strengths.
Child

I feel like my grades define me as a person.
Child

What is the problem?

Problem 1: Knowledge and content needs redesigning

Content and diversity

Lewis Howard Latimer was born on 4 September 1848 and died on 11 December 1928. If you were educated in the UK, you probably don't know about Lewis Latimer and his legacy. I didn't. If you are an educator and you are reading this book, please go and look up his name on Google. I don't need to school you on how to gain knowledge, but the knowledge you are directed to gain is vitally important. Why?

The Black Panther Party was a revolutionary socialist organisation founded in 1966 in Oakland, California, by Huey Newton and Bobby Seale. The movement emerged in response to systemic racism, police brutality, and economic inequality faced by Black communities in the United States. Initially established to monitor police activity and prevent violence against Black citizens, the party quickly expanded its mission to include community empowerment programmes such as free breakfasts for children, health clinics, and education initiatives.

I recently read a book by Michael Holding, *Why We Kneel, How We Rise*, who stresses the point of education in relation to creating an anti-racist society, and world. I learned so many things that I didn't know about Black heroes, people who were not brought into the "curriculum" when I was a child, and to a greater extent, still aren't. Why?

My husband often talks about his experiences of education, particularly through later primary school and his experience in secondary school in the UK, a Black male growing up in the working-class white suburbs. Imagine if he had the strength of these heroes behind him when he was being called the "N word", fighting back and being isolated for doing so. Imagine if those around him were educated to understand their own bias and racial prejudice in those moments.

The lack of curriculum diversity is just one of the many issues with relating to what we teach in the UK. It sits alongside relevance of content for the 21st century learner, starting with understanding the need for knowledge and how this is obtained for the 2025 learner.

Knowledge

The gaining of knowledge has moved on from the 1990s. (I use this as a reference, because it was when I experienced the education system.) We have the internet, and the artificial intelligence (AI) movement is taking us even further into a world of knowledge being available at our fingertips. A lesson on Henry VIII can be self-taught in seconds via the use of AI. I wondered about the way we teach and what we teach in schools, and whether anyone has stopped to think about the relevance of a lesson, or how it could be taught differently and in far greater depth, to foster inquiry skills, oracy skills, social communication skills, and motivation for learning.

Only if the child is motivated by what they are learning will they possibly then seek reinforcement of facts and knowledge through self-study.

In my late 20s I worked in a school in East London, a high-achieving secondary school within a poor district, predominantly with students from various ethnic minority backgrounds, whose value on education was high, given that in this country, unlike their home country, education is free! I had a brilliant job title, "Aim Higher and Destinations Coordinator", which basically meant I had the opportunity to support kids with a pathway for post 16, not just year 11 but across the whole school. The fact this post was even created tells you something about the innovative Headteacher at the time!

I'll never forget the story Adib (alias), head boy, told me about his English lesson. He came into my office especially excited to tell me about the lesson he just took part in. I don't recall if it was English or History, but the content was linked to the air raids during World War II. Adib and his peers had entered the room, which was dark and silent, desks overturned and draped with cloth to make small gaps for the children to come in and hide under. The teacher had turned the class into an air raid shelter and read a chapter of a book whilst getting children to play various parts, enacting the resonance of the feelings and fear of the sirens.

Wow – what a great teacher! I bet those kids will never forget that lesson, that book chapter, and that learning. That class did not need to know the facts about air raid shelters and World War II – they could get that from Google, or these days ChatGPT. What they were given that day was an understanding of the human experiences of the war, the emotions, the fear, the heroism. If we connect with what we are learning on an emotional level, we will seek out the facts ourselves. Are our children connected with what they are learning?

Problem 2: Children are not connected with what they are learning

When you ask children about what they want to learn, their requests are consistently clear, their awareness of the "teach to test" curriculum is evident, as are their preferences in curriculum delivery:

- *"I want to go on trips and have people come to school and teach things our teachers aren't expert in. Like writers and illustrators and dancers. I want to be able to express myself more in what I can wear and be proud of myself, not just the same as everyone else."*
- *"Too much exam pressure and revision."*
- *"Well it's ok because they don't make the lesson fun. They are trying to make the lesson fun but it is not that fun. Some of the lessons are ok."*
- *"The teachers are trying to do too much, way too fast for the average student in a lot of the lessons."*

Secondary school pupils also highlighted a desire for their learning and lessons to be linked to their future and be supportive of them progressing into adulthood. In particular, a focus was placed on life skills such as understanding tax and being able to budget and not solely focusing on lessons to get them through exams:

- *"The things I am learning in school are mostly for my upcoming GCSE and I feel like I would be great if we learned other things about what life would be like after school."*
- *"More life lessons that will help in actual life."*
- *"Learn how to manage your money, how to get a job, how to pay bills, how to buy a house."*
- *"Learn survival skills (how to make a fire, what to do if you are kidnapped etc)."*
- *"In maths it's irrelevant to my life."*

During the pupil views project (Popoola and Sivers, 2021; Popoola and Sivers, 2023; Sivers et al., 2022), the idea of curriculum continued to arise in the narrative. For example, when we asked children what they had missed about school, the elements of the curriculum that were mentioned were those that were practical, social, and generally those we would consider to be "enrichment":

- *"I miss PE and running around with all my friends. I miss cooking and things to do with my hands."*
- *"Hobbies that I like doing such as Art, the subject really interests me and I wish I could do more."*
- *"We also need more fun lessons like food tech or PE."*

Others talked about the experience at home during the Covid-19 lockdown, some in a more positive way than others. For example, one child said: *"I liked that, at home, I could learn other things that we don't do at school. I also had two hours on my bike or playing everyday. In the first lockdown I did 1000 km on my bike."*

In such a changing world, we have to ask ourselves if our curriculum and the delivery of it are relevant to the 21st century learner. The technological revolution over the past 20 years has propelled us into a world where knowledge is instantaneous and we can learn whatever we like, whenever we like. The point is, we need to think more about sparking interest, motivation, and igniting the mind to "want to know". Based on how the majority of children experience school, we are doing the opposite. When we get frustrated with children's lack of interest, with their "behaviour" as a result of disengagement, we divert quickly to our behaviourist psychology for answers and try to scare them into exhibiting good "behaviours for learning". Maybe we should think more about why a child would be disengaged from school? What are we doing wrong?

Problem 3: Behaviourist and outdated psychology

Teaching through rewards and sanctions is outdated. We know more about child development now, and yet the school system refuses to catch up. I genuinely believe we are creating angry children, through the lens of angry adults, who are frustrated with the lack of autonomy and creativity in their own jobs, teaching to test, spending their time giving out green and red points, detentions, "on calls". Who would enjoy being a teacher these days, with the layers of pressure and targets, data drops galore, constant changes in inspection frameworks, safeguarding, attendance, and results, results, results?

Paul Dix's *When the Adults Change, Everything Changes* is one of my favourite books on the topic of school-wide behaviour. It highlights the belief that through creating punishment and reward systems we are creating consistency in expectations. This belief is false. What is red to me may be pink to you; the subjective human is not able to be consistent in their expectations if the expectations are only laid out in red and green points on a clever app that goes home to parents for some good old "double punishment". Dix dispels the consistency myth, pointing out that the only way to create safety and consistency for children is when they "know what to expect from adults": consistent language, consistent adult behaviours, based on compassion and kindness, whilst remaining firm about the expectations of being good humans, being kind to each other, and kind to oneself.

Three examples of difference from around the world

The new curriculum for Wales

In 2022, Wales initiated a comprehensive overhaul of its education system with the introduction of the Curriculum for Wales. This reform aims to provide a more holistic and flexible learning experience for students aged 3 to 16. The traditional key stages have been replaced by seamless learning progression, and subjects are now organised into six Areas of Learning and Experience:

1. Languages, Literacy, and Communication
2. Mathematics and Numeracy
3. Science and Technology
4. Health and Wellbeing
5. Humanities
6. Expressive Arts

This structure is designed to foster interdisciplinary learning and equip students with skills relevant to the 21st century. While GCSEs remain part of the assessment framework, they have been adapted to align with the new curriculum's objectives.

Research into the early implementation of the Curriculum for Wales indicates a positive shift towards more dynamic and engaging teaching practices. A study published in 2023 highlights that schools are embracing the curriculum's flexibility, allowing educators to tailor learning experiences to their students' needs. This adaptability has been linked to increased student engagement and a deeper understanding of subject matter. However, the research also emphasises the necessity for ongoing support and professional development for teachers to fully realize the curriculum's potential.

Additionally, the Welsh Government has committed to continuous evaluation of the curriculum's impact. Ongoing research, initiated in autumn 2022, aims to monitor the reforms' progress in practice and identify areas requiring additional support. This proactive approach ensures that the curriculum evolves in response to feedback from educators and students, promoting a culture of continuous improvement within the Welsh education system.

The Curriculum for Wales represents a significant step forward in modernising education, with early findings suggesting benefits in teaching methodologies and student engagement.

The Finnish education system

It is no secret if you work in the world of education that the Finnish school system is the envy of the community. I often wonder why, when we have an example of a state getting it right, that we don't just copy and paste their model. Finland is the number 1 country in the UN happiness index (as of

2025) and is one of a few countries with the highest levels of adult literacy in the world. The Finnish Government has also recently boasted that they are close to eradicating homelessness.

Teachers in Finland have a five-year programme of teaching qualification and high school teachers are educated to master's level in their specialist subject and are required to write an experimental research paper that will contribute to the evidence base of the profession. Teaching is a high-status profession and all teachers are expected to contribute to the development of the curriculum, making it a "bottom-up" design, created by those delivering it rather than being dictated by central government. Joint decision-making is fundamental and teacher's report having high autonomy in their work.

The Finnish system is underpinned by the belief that education is an instrument to balance social inequality, and values fairness, trust, and honesty. Children in Finnish schools all receive a free, good-quality meal as part of their school day, and have access to healthcare, including counselling/welfare. Individuality is highly promoted. In Finland, children start school at 7 years old, and they play. Children have free reign in the developing childhood years, and the focus is on creative play. Learning is not siloed into "phonics time", "numeracy hour", or any other formal term. Yet, children in Finland have excellent levels of literacy and numeracy, without the need for formalised "lessons". The Finnish believe that social skills are the key learning priority for children.

In upper secondary school, Finnish pupils are valued for their individual skills, and have the opportunity to follow vocational pathways at post 16 if they do not want to attend university. This is a similar trend to the UK system, which enables young adults to go, after their GCSEs, to college to study for qualifications that will get them into university, or study more vocational courses and apprenticeships that will lead them into a career. The key difference is not the pathway, but the value placed on both pathways in Finland, which is equal. During their secondary phase, students report feeling supported to find their way through skills development and more personalised learning and self-directed pathways.

We can see from pupil voice in the UK that the message about obtaining GCSEs is much more narrow: if you don't pass them, with a grade 4 or above, you're a failure. This pressure comes from the competitive nature of the UK school system. Schools are frequently compared and judged on academic results, both in league tables and by Ofsted. In Finland, competition between pupils and schools does not exist; in fact, collaboration between pupils on projects that bring out their individual strengths is encouraged, as is collaboration around good practice for schools. Research into the impact of highly competitive environments forms the basis of this ethos; comparison promotes interpersonal factors such as low self-esteem and self-worth.

Finally, in Finland school starts later, between 9am and 10am depending on the school and the day. I have been experiencing the challenges of timing of the school day in recent months: the sleep cycle of the teenager! Recent developments in neuroscience have informed us that when a child hits puberty, their brain initiates a "rewire", predominantly due to hormonal changes that alter the brain's chemistry. One of the key changes is sleep.

The sleep hormone that aids sleep in all humans is called melatonin, a term that is likely to be familiar to many educators because of the rise in children being prescribed melatonin to support good sleep. Melatonin in a child entering puberty shifts from being relatively high at nighttime to extremely low due to the other hormonal changes happening simultaneously. In contrast, melatonin is extremely high in the morning, for these children entering puberty, which is why the sleep cycle of the teenager is so different to that of younger children or adults. This regulates itself as the child gets older, but this is another example of how the school system in the UK is created in opposition of scientific knowledge.

The school day in the UK has been getting progressively earlier and earlier, with some schools starting as early as 8:20am. Sleep research also tells us that sleep is highly associated with academic outcomes, due to the impact on attention and focus. I wonder what the impact on our GCSEs would be if the UK school day shifted to start later and finish later in the day? Well, we know, based on research in the UK, that a later school start time, particularly for teenagers, can significantly improve sleep duration, attendance, alertness in class, academic performance, and overall wellbeing, with studies showing positive correlations between later start times and reduced rates of illness.

The International Baccalaureate (IB)

In my mid to late 20s, circa 2008, I spent almost three years working in Shanghai, China. I worked in a primary school, teaching art for children aged 5–12. The school was "bilingual", meaning each class had both an English-speaking (English as a first language) and a Chinese (Mandarin as a first language) teacher – a model that meant teaching was accessible and children were enriched in both languages, regardless of their own first language. It was an international school that followed the Primary Years Program (PYP) of the IB.

At the time of working at the school, my interest in pedagogy and understanding the impact of curriculum was superseded by, well, being in my 20s. I wish I had paid more attention, but what I do remember is the focus on "inquiry-based learning". The language around learning was unique, based on a life-long learning journey for everyone, promoting critical thinking. The curriculum is designed around three learning pillars: the learner, teaching, and the learning community.

The learner

The students were all encouraged to understand and reflect on their "learner profile", which was based on these ten key constructs:

1. Inquirers
2. Knowledgeable
3. Thinkers
4. Communicators
5. Principled
6. Open-minded
7. Caring
8. Risk-takers
9. Balanced
10. Reflective

The overarching statement, taken from the IB learner profile (IB Organization, 2013), is: "the aim of all IB programs is to create internationally minded people, who, recognising their common humanity and shared guardianship of the planet, help to create a better and more peaceful world". Wow!

Teaching

The teaching within the PYP is a blend of knowledge and concept-driven inquiry. Children are given knowledge, and then a conceptual inquiry approach is used as a powerful vehicle for learning that values concepts and promotes meaning and understanding. It challenges students to engage critically and creatively with significant ideas beyond the surface level of knowing. PYP teachers use powerful, broad, and abstract concepts as a lens to organise learning within units of inquiry and subject-specific learning.

I remember children creating a range of ways to organise their learning, often using multimedia presentation and portfolio.

The development of collaboration was enhanced through the group inquiry-based projects. Oracy skills were continually refined through presentations to the rest of the class, teachers, and, regularly, parents. The curriculum was also transdisciplinary, which meant children had the opportunity to connect ideas and learning across subjects, and were driven by their own interests within a subject or topic, giving room for autonomy and building competence. Furthermore, the IB aims to develop approaches to learning skills for children, skills that are grounded in the belief that "learning how to learn" is fundamental to humanity both inside and outside of school. The "approaches to learning skills" are:

- Thinking skills
- Research skills
- Communication skills
- Self-management skills
- Social skills

The learning community

The world is an essential resource within the IB curriculum and children are taught to think broadly and outside of their own existence, with importance placed on humanity and citizenship. The learning community ethos promotes belonging for all students, their families, all staff who work in the organisation, and other important adults who influence the students' lives.

What now for the UK curriculum?

In 2023 I took part in a conference called "Rethinking Education". My colleague Sarah Sivers and I presented our work on pupil views through the pandemic to a small group of delegates. The conference was a collection of voices, organised by the brilliant Dr James Mannion (leader of this movement/organisation), people who have new ideas about how we can improve the current system, and what needs to change to end the current "attendance crisis", the high rates of exclusion, and the disaffection and disconnection between children and their education.

The new Labour government has more recently launched a review into the curriculum, asking those in the field to comment and respond on challenges and problems of curriculum design and content. The Review Panel published an interim report in March 2025, which suggested that while things were felt to be broadly working well, there was a great diversity in the views shared around curriculum and assessment arrangements. The Review Panel also highlighted areas of focus for the next phase of the review in terms of opportunities and improvement. This includes an acknowledgement that the system is not working well for all, that the curriculum content is inhibiting learning and is not inclusive, that the curriculum needs to respond to social and technological change, and to review post 16 pathways.

Change is unlikely to be imminent, and can only successfully be done over a period of time. But we cannot continue to deliver schooling in the way we are doing now – the risk and stakes are too high.

Change!

I'd like to start with the psychology of motivation, Self-Determination Theory (SDT, Deci and Ryan, 2001), a theory used by many psychologists and authors in recent years to highlight the reasons for a lack of motivation in children to learn. SDT highlights three core constructs that interact to create a learner who is self-motivated.

1. **Autonomy:** the freedom to choose what we are learning or teaching and have agency over our work
2. **Competence:** feeling able, knowing our strengths
3. **Relatedness:** gaining satisfaction through working with others towards a common goal

Think about the concept of autonomy in relation to our current school system. I have a son who is 3 years old who has all the autonomy in the world in his early years setting: free play, choice over which toys to play with, very little adult direction, learning through play. I also have a child who is 13. She is prevented from using the bathroom when she needs it (very difficult during menstruation), her socks must be the correct length, her shirt tucked in, timetables set, content delivered by scheme of work, reading time imposed, seating plans arranged. Autonomy in our secondary education is minimal.

Think about the idea of competence in our current school system. The voices of children tell us that they know importance is placed on passing

GCSEs, but mainly the system is set up to promote the importance of English, Maths and (perhaps slightly less so) Science. Children are "taught to test" with very little room for exploration of individual interest within a subject, individual opinions and ideas, and certainly minimal exploration of relevance to the world. **Many children are being disaffected by the curriculum because they do not see themselves in it.** This links back to the content challenges raised around equality and diversity, but also to competence. If I am not good at Maths or English, I am not good.

Consider the concept of relatedness within motivation. My first ever part-time job when I turned 16 was in a local "chippy" (fish and chip takeaway). I think I was paid around £2.10 per hour and the nights were long and late. I had to wear a straw hat with a blue and white ribbon tied around the top of the rim. I kept the job because the people I worked for and with were great. We laughed and enjoyed our time together, and this was my single motivation for stinking of chip fat two nights a week. My daughter is a social being. She "hates" school and everything about it. But I am a lucky parent who does not have to manage the complexities of school attendance, because she goes to be with her peers.

The benefits of inquiry-based learning and what this could look like in UK schools

The three examples of difference given above all have a common theme of increased autonomy for their learners, whether this is in the way the curriculum is delivered, how the children learn, or the content itself. One key factor underpinning all of the examples above is the concept of inquiry-based learning that is led by child interest. Knowledge will always remain important to "give" to children, because interest needs to be sparked by a concept, a challenge, or an idea, and without knowledge of the world such questions are difficult to raise.

However, it would not be massively inconceivable to imagine a curriculum that allowed for some self-directed project work that is underpinned by the development concepts within the IB programme. I wonder whether in the UK this could initially be divided into a percentage of learning. Project pathways would enable children to develop their understanding of cross-curricular ideas, possibly linked to what they have already learned in other subjects and based on their learning questions from some of the key knowledge they have been taught. Project work would either be individual, and student-led, where this is the preference for the child based on their project, or alternatively would be a group project.

Group projects are a brilliant tool for motivating students. The "relatedness" mechanism within Self-Determination Theory comes into play here: as humans we are consistently more motivated when working as part of a group towards a shared purpose and outcomes. This can be difficult for children who need support with social relationships, but therefore even more of a reason to incorporate group work with guidance from adults. Relationships are an essential part of any job role. I often say to people that 90% of my role as a leader is about managing relationship dynamics, the other 10% being a mix of specialist expertise, organisation skills, creativity, and public speaking.

Within any job role, managing social relationships with colleagues can be the difference between success and lack thereof. Research (Riggio et al., 2020) tells us that if you can work as part of a team, understand the perspective of others, and manage your own emotions, you are more likely to be successful in the workplace, and Individuals proficient in these areas are more likely to navigate complex work environments successfully, leading to career advancement and enhanced organisational effectiveness. This highlights the importance of school playing a role in fostering these skills as an embedded part of the curriculum.

Outcomes of projects can also support the development of a range of skills that are needed to be successful in the workplace. For example, developing oracy skills in children yields numerous benefits across academic, social, and emotional domains. Research indicates that a strong command of spoken language enhances reading comprehension and overall literacy. Socially, oracy education fosters self-esteem and confidence, enabling children to articulate their thoughts and engage in meaningful discussions. Engaging in high-quality oracy practices during lessons deepens understanding and is linked with improved test scores and exam grades, as well as greater knowledge retention, vocabulary acquisition, and reasoning skills. Furthermore, oracy contributes to self-regulation and empathy. Children use private speech to guide their behaviour and attention, aiding in emotional regulation and problem-solving. This self-directed speech helps them manage emotions and navigate social interactions effectively.

Using student-led project work to encourage public speaking and presentation skills is another benefit of inquiry-based learning. Again, thinking about skills for the future, public speaking is widely recognised as a critical skill for career advancement. Individuals proficient in public speaking often experience enhanced visibility within their organisations, leading to recognition and potential promotions. Conversely, those who avoid public speaking may face limitations in career progression, as effective communication is essential in many professional roles. Developing public speaking skills can boost confidence, improve overall communication abilities, and open opportunities for leadership positions.

Developing a sense of competence and relatedness through inquiry-based learning

In the world of mental health, we often talk about resilience and wellbeing. In the city in which I work, we have high numbers of children who are subject to Adverse Childhood Experiences (ACEs). One of the things that we often think about is outcomes for children who have been through challenging environments, particularly those who have been taken into the care system, and what the factors are for those who have better outcomes. Something that is a common factor, alongside others, is whether a child has a sense of competence and identity through such competence. For example, a child might have a particular talent or skills that enable them to have an outlet, whether that be creative or physical.

Competence in the current system is low for children who are not able to fit. Competence at both academic subjects and being part of the social world is low for children who either struggle with academics or with regulating emotions (which in turn impacts on behaviour). A child who is struggling with either of these things will tell you, *"They hate me, I hate school, I'm thick, I rubbish at . . .".*

This is of course linked to inclusion and ensuring every child is recognised for their brilliance. But in a narrow knowledge-based and teach-to-test curriculum, there is little room for exploration of self and individual strengths. Nor are such things credited, because the language in schools is all geared towards passing those core subjects, and this is then what is internalised as success.

Inquiry-based learning alongside a knowledge-rich and content-relevant curriculum would allow all children to take something they are curious about, learn more about it independently, ask their own questions, and find ways to make their learning meaningful, and also work as part of a team. The skills rewarded also create differences in attributions of success. What if we shifted the idea of success to the individual personal attributes identified in the IB learner profile? What if these were the things being pointed out by teachers as being the components of an effective learner?

An example of how to implement an inquiry-based project

Managing finance is a key idea that children often talk about when they are asked what they want to learn in school, e.g. *"How does tax work and how do I set up a business?"* The example below is based on the IB process of inquiry-based learning.

Inquiry-based project example: "Making smart financial choices"

Transdisciplinary theme: How we organise ourselves

Central idea: Managing finances effectively helps individuals and communities make informed decisions.

Lines of inquiry:

1. The role of money in daily life and society
2. Financial decision-making and its impact
3. Strategies for budgeting, saving, and spending wisely

Stages of the inquiry-based project (using the PYP IB Inquiry Cycle)
Tuning in (provocation and engagement):

- *Provocation activity:* present students with different scenarios, e.g. a person receives money as a gift, someone wants to buy a toy but has limited funds. Ask: *What would you do? Why?*
- *Discussion:* use a *See–Think–Wonder* routine with images of people spending, saving, and budgeting.

Finding out (exploration and research):

- *Guest speaker:* invite a financial expert, entrepreneur, or bank representative to discuss the importance of budgeting and saving.
- *Interactive activities:*
    - Role-playing game where students are given an imaginary budget and must make spending choices
    - Math integration, which uses practice adding, subtracting, and calculating percentages for savings and expenses

- *Research task:* students investigate the differences between needs and wants, saving versus spending, and different forms of currency (cash, digital, credit)

Sorting out (analysing and organising information):

- *Group collaboration:*
    - Create mind maps showing how money is earned, spent, saved, and donated
    - Compare financial habits of different cultures and societies
- *Financial decision-making activity:*
    - Students plan a family budget for one month, considering expenses like rent, food, transport, and entertainment
    - Students research real-life costs and discuss financial priorities

Going further (application and action):

- *Student inquiry project:*
    - Students choose a financial topic (e.g. saving for the future, managing a small business, smart spending) and present key takeaways
- *Entrepreneurial challenge:*
    - In groups, students develop a small business idea with a budget, pricing strategy, and financial plan
    - Students present their business ideas in a *Shark Tank* style event

Taking action (applying learning to the real world):

- *Showcase and reflection:*
    - Students create financial literacy posters or videos for younger students
    - Students organise a classroom or school charity fundraiser, applying financial management principles

- *Personal action plan:*
    - Each student sets a financial goal, e.g. saving a certain amount of money, making informed spending choices
    - Students reflect on their learning journey and how they will use financial skills in the future

Assessment and reflection:

- *Formative:* teacher observations, student journals, peer discussions, and real-life budgeting activities
- *Summative:* students create a financial plan, present their budgeting project, or run a small business simulation
- *Self-assessment:* students reflect on what they have learned and how they can apply financial skills in real life.

Over the course of their project, you can see the vast array of skills that students would learn, alongside gaining knowledge. Other areas of curriculum are pulled in and utilised, and students start to see the purpose in gaining maths skills, for example, and how to apply such skills to real-world scenarios.

Final thoughts

The curriculum is an essential tool for creating happy learners, and happy learners are much more likely to be successful. When asked about what they are learning, children clearly note the irrelevance and painstaking impact of the current teach-to-test model. The pressure of exams and continual "get good grades" discourse has an impact on children's mental health. The curriculum is one essential element of change that is therefore needed if we are to meaningfully "reimagine schools for the 21st century". I posit that, by bringing in a percentage of time for inquiry-based project work, underpinned by the psychology of motivation, and learning from the excellent systems created in other countries, we could make a difference to so many children who are struggling to fit, feeling incompetent, feeling the pressure, and voting with their feet and not attending school at all.

Key takeaways

1. Children are disconnected from an outdated and rigid curriculum. Many students report feeling disengaged from a curriculum focused on rote learning and test performance. There is a strong desire for more practical, life-relevant skills such as financial literacy, managing emotions, and understanding real-world contexts. Current educational practices often ignore the interests and lived experiences of children, contributing to disengagement and reduced motivation (Deci and Ryan, 2001; Popoola and Sivers, 2021, 2023).
2. Global examples show the value of autonomy and inquiry-based learning. The chapter highlights successful education systems, such as Finland and the International Baccalaureate (IB), which emphasise child-led inquiry, autonomy, and holistic skill development. These systems reduce competition and focus on building social, emotional, and cognitive competencies, which enhances both academic and personal growth (IB, 2022; United Nations, 2023).
3. The psychology of motivation must underpin curriculum reform. The application of Self-Determination Theory (Deci and Ryan, 2001) suggests that autonomy, competence, and relatedness are critical to student motivation and success. UK schools currently limit student autonomy and competence by focusing on narrow academic outcomes. Incorporating inquiry-based learning and project work into the curriculum could significantly enhance engagement, confidence, and life-long learning skills.

References

Deci, E.L. and Ryan, R.M., 2001. Self-Determination Theory: Perspective on motivation in education. *Educational Psychologist*, 26(3–4), pp. 325–346.

Dix, P., 2017. *When the Adults Change, Everything Changes: Seismic Shifts in School Behaviour.* Carmarthen: Crown House Publishing.

Holding, M., 2021. *Why We Kneel, How We Rise.* London: Simon & Schuster.

International Baccalaureate (IB), 2022. *Primary Years Programme: A Basis for Learning.* Geneva: International Baccalaureate Organization.

IB Organization, 2013. *IB Learner Profile Booklet*. Geneva: International Baccalaureate Organization.

Ofsted, 2022. *School Inspection Handbook*. Manchester: Office for Standards in Education.

Popoola, M. and Sivers, S., 2021. Hearing the voices of children and young people: An ecological systems analysis of individual difference and experiences during the Covid-19 lockdown. *DECP Debate*, 177, pp. 21–25.

Popoola, M. and Sivers, S., 2023. Maslow, relationships and square pegs. In F. Morgan and E. Costello (Eds.), *Square Pegs: Inclusivity, Compassion and Fitting In – A Guide for Schools* (pp. 77–88). Wales: Independent Thinking Press.

Review Panel, 2025. *Curriculum and Assessment Review: Interim Report*. London: Crown Copyright.

Riggio, R.E., Zhu, W., and Reina, C.S., 2020. The role of social skills in the development of leader competencies. *Journal of Leadership Studies*, 14(1), pp. 6–14.

Sivers, S., Wendland, S., Baggley, L., and Boyle, K., 2022. What children and young people told us as the Covid-19 pandemic unfolded. In C. Arnold and B. Davis (Eds.), *Children in Lockdown: Learning the Lessons of Pandemic Times*. London: Karnac.

Sleep Foundation, 2023. Teen sleep and school start times. Available at: https://www.sleepfoundation.org [Accessed 1 May 2025].

United Nations, 2023. *World Happiness Report*. New York: United Nations.

Welsh Government, 2023. *Curriculum for Wales: Research on Early Implementation*. Cardiff: Welsh Government.

6

What do children out of school say about their experiences in mainstream education?

Maddi Popoola

Sometimes I just felt overwhelmed by the amount of work and all the people at school. I just need time alone to get a break from it all. After a while I felt really low and couldn't get motivated for anything.
Child

I was always in trouble. School makes me feel like I'm a failure to my family. Makes me not want to be alive.
Child

Attendance: What is the current problem?

Why would a child not want to, or be able to, attend school? I imagine in some parts of the world where education is not free, children and parents alike would find it unimaginable that the offer of free education is not taken by all. After all, it is the key to your future, right? This is where the divide between school and education has been created in the UK, and with the statistics presented below, we have to ask ourselves, is school providing the education that our children need and deserve?

There many reasons for children not attending school, and a range of labels and acronyms that float around the world of education and "improving attendance". Some are more localised terms that have been developed through initiatives and research into understanding the aetiology of non-school attendance, and some are more well known at a national level. One such term that has certainly grown in its use is EBSA (Emotionally Based School Avoidance), and this continues to be used for many children who are unable to attend school because they are anxious and have poor mental health. The question, of course, is the chicken and egg: is school the sole cause of anxiety and, therefore, the problem? Or is the child anxious and lacking in resilience, and, therefore, is the child's mental health the problem?

Other terms that are often used if you work in a school or with a school are those set at a national level, such as PA (severely persistently absent – for any child whose attendance is below 90%), SPA (severely persistently absenteeism – for any child whose attendance is 50% or less), and the evolving term CME (which used to mean children who had gone missing from their school – children missing education – and were thought to have moved to a different area and is now more broadly used to describe any child who is not registered at school and who is not receiving suitable education otherwise). The current position in the UK is outlined in a recently published report (House of Commons Library, 2025):

Overall absence rates:

- In 2022/2023, the national absence rate for state-funded schools was 7.4%, slightly down from 7.6% in 2021/2022, but still significantly above the pre-pandemic levels (4.5–4.8% from 2013–2019).
- 2024/2025 provisional estimate: 6.5% overall; 8.0% in secondary, 5.2% in primary, and 12.7% in special schools.

Persistent and severe absence (House of Commons Library, 2025):

- In 2022/2023, 21.2% of pupils were persistently absent (missed ≥10% of sessions), around 1.6 million pupils.
- Severely absent (≥50% absence): 2.0% of pupils, around 150,000 pupils.
- Pre-pandemic (2018/19) persistent absence was 10.9%, showing absence has almost doubled.

Vulnerable groups (House of Commons Library, 2025):

- Free School Meals (FSM): 36.5% persistent absence (vs 15.6% for non-FSM).
- Special Educational Needs (SEN) with Education, Health, and Care Plans (EHCPs): 36% persistently absent, 12.3% absence rate.

- Gypsy/Roma: 64.9% persistent absence.
- Traveller of Irish Heritage: 72% persistent absence.
- Lowest absence among Chinese students (3.4%).

Currently, based on the most recent live data in the UK, the PA rate for the academic year 2024/2025 in the UK is 18.4%, with the number of CME children standing at 39,200.

How can we make sense of data to help us understand barriers to school attendance?

Data and research are essential in helping us to understand the problem with school attendance. One way to think about the factors that contribute to non-school attendance is to consider the predisposing (most at risk because of a range of personal, family, or other circumstances), precipitating (sudden or traumatic life events), and maintaining factors (circumstances and behaviours that prolong and lead to feeling of stuck-ness). Further to this, such factors can be divided between those linked to school, the child themselves, and the family. Examples are provided below.

Some of the barriers to attendance linked to school ethos and environment:

- Changes to friendship groups and bullying (precipitating)
- Poor school belonging and connectedness (precipitating)
- Transition to secondary school, between key stages or change of school (precipitating)
- Structure of school day (precipitating and maintaining where change isn't an option)
- Academic demands/high levels of pressure and performance-orientated classrooms (precipitating and maintaining)
- Journey to school (precipitating)
- Exams (precipitating and maintaining)
- Peer or staff relationships, e.g. lack of kindness and compassion, including bullying (precipitating and maintaining)
- School phase, e.g. transitions, added pressure due to exams (precipitating)
- School size and sensory environment, e.g. loudness/busyness (precipitating and maintaining)
- School climate or culture (precipitating and maintaining)

Some of the barriers or at-risk factors linked to the child:

- The most at-risk ages and their corresponding year groups are:
    - Year 1 (ages 5–6)
    - Year 7 (ages 11–12)
    - Year 9 (ages 13–14)
- This is a predisposing characteristic
- Fear of failure and poor self-confidence (maintaining)
- Special educational needs and disabilities (SEND): learning difficulties, developmental problems, or autism spectrum condition especially if unidentified or unsupported (predisposing)
- Separation anxiety from parent (maintaining)
- Traumatic events: bereavement/transition or change/separation (precipitating and maintaining).
- Emotional regulation skills/emotional literacy (predisposing)
- History of mental health difficulties (predisposing)

Some of the barriers or at-risk factors linked to the family:

- Changes in family dynamics: birth of sibling, separation (precipitating)
- Family history of psychiatric or medical difficulties (predisposing)
- Parent physical and mental health problems (predisposing, maintaining)
- Dysfunctional family interactions and safeguarding concerns (predisposing, precipitating, and maintaining)
- Loss and bereavement (precipitating)
- Poverty (predisposing and maintaining)
- High levels of family stress (precipitating and maintaining)
- Young carers (predisposing)
- Ethnicity and culture, e.g. differing levels of importance placed on education based on culture (predisposing)

Some further maintaining factors that are often caused by the absence itself are:

- The cycle of reinforcement (when we feel anxious, the thing that makes us feel anxious is avoided and the avoidance creates a reduction in anxiety, which then reinforces the behaviour of avoidance)

- A breakdown of trust between the family and school
- Sleep cycles and routines are disturbed (often gaming late into the night)
- Social embarrassment of returning
- Worrying about missed learning
- Waiting lists for help

With so many contributing risk factors and potential barriers, it is important schools don't make any conclusions about "the problem" without some thorough investigation and understanding of the child and their family. The school and the school system must also be able to turn the mirror on itself and ask, what can we do better and differently? Before we explore some of the good practices making a difference and effective interventions, it is essential to understand the problem from the voices of children who are not in mainstream education for a variety of reasons.

What do children say is the problem?

In 2024, we created a survey that was sent to local and national organisations for children who are not in mainstream school, e.g. those who are home educated, those who are in alternative education settings due to exclusion, and those who do not currently have a school place. A breakdown of the 214 children who responded to the survey by year group is provided (4 did not respond):

- Year 6: 14 respondents
- Year 7: 29 respondents
- Year 8: 41 respondents
- Year 9: 49 respondents
- Year 10: 61 respondents
- Year 11: 20 respondents

The current education status of respondents was as follows (including 1 duplication):

- Home educated: 130 respondents
- Attending an alternative school or provision: 51 respondents
- Out of school or "other": 38 respondents

Those who answered "out of school or other" were then asked to elaborate, with comments to further describe and explain their current education status. From the 38 who ticked this option, 36 provided further elaboration and commentary, and a grouping analysis was done on the data, finding key themes for education status.

Unmet special educational needs and disabilities (SEND):

- Many families report that children's needs (often linked to autism, ADHD, ODD, sensory processing issues, etc.) were not met in mainstream or specialist settings.
- Several children were excluded or placed on reduced timetables due to behavioural or emotional regulation challenges linked to their conditions.
- Some children were on the pathway for diagnosis, but support was not in place pre-diagnosis, causing deterioration in mental health and educational engagement.

Examples:

Waiting on autism and ADHD testing . . .

Parent

Not receiving the correct support in school setting

Parent

No special school could meet need . . .

Parent

School weren't delivering, Local Authority [LA] weren't holding school to account . . .

Parent

Inappropriate school placements:

- Multiple families mention being on roll at schools (mainstream or special) that do not meet the child's needs, resulting in non-attendance despite support from the setting.
- Some explicitly state that no suitable provision exists in their area.

Examples:

No school to meet needs . . .

                                                                                           Parent

Not suited in special school . . .

                                                                                            Parent

LA agree school settings not appropriate . . .

                                                                                           Parent

Lack of provision or delays from the local authority:

- Many respondents highlight long waits for EHCPs, incomplete provision, or lack of follow-up from the LA.
- Several mention being on roll but receiving no education for long periods.

Examples:

My school placement ceased . . . the LA hasn't provided anything since . . .

                                                                                           Parent

Still on roll . . . but no education provided for 2.5 years.

                                                                                           Parent

Awaiting EHCP final draft . . .

                                                                                           Parent

Alternative provision and EOTAS (Education Other Than at School):

- A notable number of families are accessing EOTAS, often reluctantly or temporarily while seeking suitable school placements.
- Packages are often piecemeal or insufficient, with many relying heavily on parents or tutors.

Examples:

EOTAS through EHCP . . .

                                                                                           Parent

Online school . . . not attended since Jan 23.

Parent

Have a tutor for 10 hours a week . . .

Parent

Elective home education (often due to lack of options):

- Some children/families have chosen to home educate, but in many cases this appears to be forced or reluctant, rather than a positive choice.
- These families often still seek LA support, school reintegration, or a future placement.

Examples:

Home educated after a stressful transition . . .

Parent

College home ed.

Parent

Currently home educating but awaiting . . .

Parent

Summary of findings of reasons for not being in education:

- **SEND-related unmet need** (especially undiagnosed or unsupported autism/attention deficit hyperactivity disorder [ADHD]) is the most commonly cited root cause.
- **Mental health issues**, including anxiety and trauma from school, are widespread.
- **Local authority failings** in EHCP processes and placement decisions frequently lead to long-term non-attendance.
- Many children are left with **no suitable or sustainable educational option**, leading to reliance on **EOTAS, tutoring, or home education**.
- There is clear **demand for flexible, personalised, and trauma-informed provision**, especially for autistic pupils and those with co-occurring mental health needs.

The next question in the survey asked children about their reasons for not attending school. Children were asked to select statements that they felt related to them/their situation, and were able to tick more than one. The answers were:

- Feeling anxious – 20%
- Didn't feel supported – 20%
- Bullied – 8.2%
- Excluded – 4.1%
- Behaviour issues – 9.5%
- Didn't fit in – 12.8%
- Strict rules – 7.2%
- Felt under pressure – 12.1%
- Work too difficult – 6.2%

The next question in the survey asked children to expand on their answers: "If you have selected one or more of the above, we would like to understand more about this and your experience. Please tell us how this felt for you." A thematic analysis of answers was then completed, with the results summarised here.

Emotional distress and mental health

Many children expressed overwhelming anxiety and emotional dysregulation related to attending school. This distress was often exacerbated by sensory overload, social challenges, or trauma. Key quotes include:

- *"The thought of going to school made me feel sick and anxious."*
- *"My anxiety about school was so bad I didn't want to be here any more."*
- *"Mainstream school caused anxiety . . . I had to hold everything in until I got home."*

Subthemes include:

- Panic attacks and physical symptoms (nausea, exhaustion)
- Fear of detentions, shouting, and punishment
- Emotional masking leading to burnout

Unmet Special Educational Needs and Disabilities (SEND)

A significant number of students reported that their autism, ADHD, or other additional needs were not understood or supported.

- *"They wanted me to be the same sort of autistic as the rest of the class."*
- *"Undiagnosed ADHD made it very difficult to deal with school I . . . in the end they gave up trying to help me."*
- *"SENCO [Special Educational Needs Coordinator] offered little real support."*

Subthemes include:

- Inappropriate settings (mainstream or specialist)
- EHCP not followed or removed
- Mislabelling of behaviour instead of recognising need

Bullying and unsafe environments

Bullying was cited frequently, along with accounts of schools failing to address it, or, in some cases, punishing the victim:

- *"I was bullied . . . school told me to be more resilient."*
- *"Bullies go unpunished . . . teachers lack respect."*
- *"The teachers even sat me next to my bully."*

Subthemes include:

- Lack of safeguarding
- Peer violence, including mention of weapons in school
- Long-term trauma from experiences

School system and environment incompatibility

Many respondents found the school environment inflexible, overstimulating, or overly rigid:

- *"Too many people, too noisy."*
- *"Strict rules, like being punished for asking questions."*
- *"Couldn't use the toilet when I needed to."*

Subthemes include:

- Sensory overload, e.g. bells, crowds, uniform discomfort
- Excessive rules without emotional support
- Detentions and isolation for neurodivergent behaviours

Academic pressure and curriculum inflexibility

Children reported either being under-stimulated or overwhelmed by academic demands:

- *"The work was often too easy or just boring."*
- *"Lessons became more about trying to control naughty students than teaching."*
- *"The pace of the lessons . . . was too high for my daughter who has dyslexia."*

Subthemes include:

- Inaccessible teaching methods
- Inability to keep up with curriculum pace
- Lack of differentiated support

Lack of autonomy and voice

Young people frequently felt excluded from decisions affecting their learning and daily life:

- *"School didn't give me the autonomy I need or involve me in decisions."*
- *"I was expected to just get on with things although I needed extra support."*
- *"Nobody listened to me."*

Trauma and physical safety concerns

Multiple accounts revealed serious trauma resulting from physical restraint, isolation, or neglect:

- *"I was sexually assaulted."*
- *"I was left in a mess after having a heavy period . . . made to stay in those clothes all day."*

Subthemes include:

- Use of restrictive practices
- Unsafe or degrading treatment
- Medical or physical needs ignored

The analysis of qualitative responses from children and families who are not attending school highlights eight key themes. The most prominent issue was severe anxiety and emotional distress, often triggered by school environments that felt overwhelming, inflexible, or unsafe. Many children experienced unmet SEND, including undiagnosed or unsupported autism and ADHD, with schools frequently failing to provide appropriate provision or implement EHCPs.

A number of young people described bullying and unsafe environments, which were often poorly managed by school staff. Others reported trauma, including physical restraint, emotional harm, and degrading incidents, leading to long-term trust issues and mental health needs.

The structure and demands of the school system were also seen as a barrier, with students citing sensory overload, strict rules, and a one-size-fits-all curriculum that did not accommodate their needs or learning styles. Children often felt excluded from decision-making and unsupported in expressing their needs, while academic pressure and a lack of differentiated support left many disengaged or falling behind.

As a result, many families have turned to home education or EOTAS, often after being failed by the system.

What did children say about what helped them in school?

The survey then asked children about what helped them in school, again giving a selection of suggestions that children could tick. The answers from 173 children were:

- Helpful and kind teachers – 22.5%
- Peer relationships – 35.3%
- Being good at something – 6%
- Having choice over what I learn – 12.1%
- Other – 23.7%

A further 165 children elaborated through qualitative comments to the comment and question: "We would like to understand more about the things that helped you in school. Please let us know what other things helped?"

Positive relationships with trusted adults:

- A consistent, understanding adult was repeatedly cited as the most important support. Young people highlighted how *"having the same teacher all the time helped me"* and how *"a key member of staff I could rely on"* made a difference.
- Kindness, calmness, and emotional safety were emphasised: *"Having a kind teacher that doesn't shout"*, *"teachers who cared about me and talked about my passions made me feel safer"*, and *"some teachers would allow a little time out to compose myself"*.

Need for emotional safety and respect:

- Many young people spoke about needing to be treated with respect and dignity: *"Respect for and from teaching staff. Being treated as another human being."* Others emphasised the importance of feeling seen and heard: *"Teachers tried to help, but it was too late"* and *"Nothing helped – school did not want to help and did not care either"*.

Autonomy and flexibility:

- A strong desire for choice and autonomy emerged: *"Being able to choose what I learn"* and *"I like to choose what I learn, but school doesn't give proper authentic choices"*.
- Students wanted a break from rigid structures: *"Being allowed to leave the classroom when I felt anxious"*, *"Having a reduced timetable"*, and *"Less children, smaller groups"*.

Peer relationships and belonging:

- Friendships were both protective and painful: *"Friends helped me in school"*, *"I had one really good friend"*, but also *"My friends changed into bullies too easily"*, and *"Now I have none"*.
- A sense of belonging and social connection was linked to positive experiences: *"Having friends and feeling part of something"*.

Practical and reasonable adjustments:

- Several young people highlighted practical tools or permissions that supported them: *"Time out cards", "Toilet pass"*, and *"Allowed to go to learning support"*.
- For others, these supports were inconsistently applied or removed: *"Had a support worker . . . but then they helped someone else"*, and *"Support changes in Year 9 meant it all fell apart"*.

The dominant message from this data is that children value **relational consistency, respect, autonomy, and emotional safety** above all. Where these were absent, even the best intentions of individual staff could not compensate for structural or cultural failings. Young people are asking to be understood, involved, and supported in ways that are responsive to their individual needs, not treated as problems to be managed.

Ways to help and examples of innovative support for children finding it difficult to attend school

The ATTEND framework (Dr Adele Tobias)

The ATTEND framework was developed by Dr Tobias (Educational Psychologist at Brighton and Hove Educational Psychology Service). During the COVID-19 pandemic, I met with the leaders of the "Square Pegs" organisation, who were working across the country with a range of parents and professionals around the issue of school attendance. Many parents were part of an organisation called "not fine in school", which remains a rapidly growing group for parents whose children are struggling to attend school. Conversations with Square Pegs gave me a sense of the enormity of the problem. Little did we know at the time that the pandemic would exacerbate what is now often termed as the "attendance crisis" (Tobias, 2022).

At this point we (myself and EP colleagues) across the country were lucky to have come across Adele's work on the ATTEND framework and get permission from Brighton and Hove to purchase the resource once it was completed, with a view to implementation and sharing findings across various EP services in the UK.

The ATTEND framework is an early intervention resource (although I have used it with a range of children at various points in their journey to some success). The framework provides schools, and those working with schools, to support children and families with a systematic way of identifying the underlying reasons for a child's absence. This is done in a collaborative way with school and parents, and as it is underpinned by relational practice and attribution theory, the ATTEND framework brings together all parties without blame, getting parents/carers, the child, and the school to work together on a joint action plan.

The initial steps are for the school to complete a series of questions about the child based on their hypothesis and views of the situation and to explore their key ideas about what the barriers are to the child attending. The barriers on the data gathering forms are grouped into sections pertaining to many of the risk, precipitating, and maintaining factors that are listed in the first part of this chapter, such as academic demand, the sensory environment, home factors, mental and physical health, etc.

The school then invites the parent in for a meeting and to complete the parent forms, which also ask a series of questions about strengths, needs, and barriers. In my experience these meetings using the ATTEND framework always bring things that were previously unknown into the room and help the school and parents reconnect in terms of developing a more shared understanding of the problem.

A third data gathering tool I included in the ATTEND framework is a child-friendly questioning exercise to gather the views of the child and find out, from their perspective, what the key barriers to attendance are.

These three pieces of data form an assessment of the problem. Schools are then further equipped to look at the situation from different perspectives, and in turn create an action plan, with identified adjustments based on an informed hypothesis from gathered data.

The action plan is co-created with the school and parents; it outlines expectations of all parties in terms of adjustments that need to be made, and some examples of adjustments are provided in the ATTEND framework. Part-time timetables often form part of reintegration, adjustments to the school day such as a slightly later start to avoid crowds, a lesson pass to leave five minutes early to avoid high traffic times in corridors, toilet pass, key adult check-ins and support, targeted interventions such as ELSA and after-school clubs, uniform adjustments, academic support where needed, support to develop social skills, or adjustments to break/lunch times with a safe space for spending unstructured times. Many of these adjustments are easily made but can make a big difference. The action plan is reviewed at regular two-week intervals and changes to provision are made in agreement with school, parents/carers, and the child.

Working with attendance can be a frustrating task; I often use the analogy of three steps forward and two back. Progress can be slow, and a tendency to rush due to the wider systemic pressures around attendance figures can prove detrimental to overall progress. I have used the ATTEND framework now in practice with several families and schools, most of which have ended in some success. Two key factors are at play when using the ATTEND framework that I believe are the mechanisms for change. The first is the removal of blame and negative attributions. In most cases, when getting involved as a psychologist, school will have assumptions about a family's lack of routine, parental and child mental health, motivation, etc. Likewise, the family will usually have negative assumptions and feelings towards the school, stating that the school are unable to meet needs, and are being inflexible. The child hears both sides and will be quick to work out how to avoid school, and what to say to ensure the blame game continues! Removing blame and working together is key to effective intervention.

The second factor is that interventions and strategies are matched to a working hypothesis based on data collection and analysis. The ATTEND framework does the "unpicking"; it helps professionals and parents/carers to get to the bottom of the problem. We often see interventions not working when they are not matched to the actual problem. Furthermore, the interventions and strategies are given a chance to work over a cycle of "plan, do, review", meaning that a graduated response is implemented and documented.

The role of Mental Health Support Teams (MHST) in supporting with Section 19 legislation and severely persistent absent children

In September 2024, the Department for Education's (DfE) *Working Together to Improve School Attendance* guidance became statutory, and with this they issued revised guidance for Arranging Education for Children Unable to Attend School for Health Reasons. As this guidance falls under the local authority's duties outlined in Section 19 of the Education Act, it was already statutory, but it refreshed the role of councils in supporting children not attending school due to their health, including their mental health, when they have been absent for 15 days or more. With the complexities of mental health, the guidance raises challenges for local authorities because: who determines if a child's mental health is the primary factor in preventing school attendance? A school is not able to make this judgement, and no guidance is provided around what or even if medical evidence is needed in such cases (DfE, 2024).

Planning for a robust response to the Section 19 pathway with limited resource continues to be a challenge for local authorities. In Nottingham we are lucky that our commissioning arrangements for the MHST mean that we have the team as a resource working within the LA rather than in a health service. Involvement of the MHST in planning for the pathway response was therefore crucial, alongside education partners and our "hospital home education" provision.

In line with our ethos of inclusion and support, we now have a dedicated team of mental health professionals working solely on the attendance pathway. A weekly expert panel screen the referrals from schools, and support is then offered by the Mental Health Support Improving Attendance Team (MIAT for short!). The MIAT is a group of qualified mental health practitioners, family support workers, and a qualified specialist practitioner. One of the shortfalls of mental health support for this cohort of children (who often find it hard to leave the house) is that the support is removed as the child is not able to access therapeutic sessions. This barrier is removed with the MIAT, who will visit children in their homes, build a relationship with the child and their family, complete an in-depth mental health and systemic assessment, and support with a graded exposure model to help the child return to school. Importantly, the support for the child is consent-based, where a child does not want to (or is unable to due to their mental health and anxiety being too extreme), the practitioners work alongside the LA to find alternative options for education, such as tutoring or alternative provision settings. This model is based on relational practice and evidence-based mental health interventions, meaning families are given the support they need to find the best outcome for the child. Schools, families, and the LA are working together under this model. Schools report feeling supported and families welcome the difference in this approach compared to more punitive ways of working. Practitioners are able to advocate for the child in terms of adjustments that need to be made. The practitioner becomes a "psychological partner" for the child and the family, developing trust and reconnecting/re-engaging the child and family with the school (Hart and Heaver, 2015).

While very much in its infancy, outcomes of the MIAT are already demonstrating change for children who haven't accessed education for two or more years. They are now finding themselves in lessons, and managing anxieties with the support of their family and school.

A key mechanism for change is the ability of practitioners to support the child and family in building resilience to anxiety. Changing the course of thought processes to language around being able to cope, being able to sit with anxiety and manage it, is a skill not just for school but for life. The MIAT intervention is also unique in ensuring all parties are brought together in the process and that schools also feel supported and develop a collaborative approach to working with the child. This is underpinned by the use of adjustments to provision for the child, which can be a challenge as a result of the wider system pressures.

The most effective intervention of all: Kindness and compassion

I recently listened to Anna Maxwell Martin on BBC Radio 4 talking about her challenges with her own child and school attendance. It was incredible to hear her raise the profile of two of the key themes that feature throughout in the voices of children who have had a negative school experience. What helps the most? "Kindness", "compassion", "a trusted adult". We often forget the power of relationships; having someone for a child is the single most protective factor for their mental health. Relationships make us feel connected, and our wellbeing is inextricably linked to our relationships. Research tells us that when a disastrous event occurs, people report that the determining factor in emotional recovery is having a community and network of people to share the experience with. In a similar vein, research into transition for school children, particularly from key stage 2–3 (primary to secondary/high school) consistently shows that the key determining factor to successful transition is peer and child–teacher relationships. Think about your own experience in school. Who was your person? Who was kind to you and made you feel worthy? Who had your back? Who championed you? (Maxwell Martin, 2024)

Adolescence is quite possibly the most difficult time of life. The biological changes alone are compelling, and this is without the additional stressors of school, the social world, and, now, a digital life. For those of us who have reached our mid-40s, our own childhood cannot be compared to that of our children. Going out without a phone, coming home when the street lights come on, no place to meet, just places to look for your mates, no apps with every minute of behaviour recorded and viewed by your parents, paper reports that required just a signature (easily faked), calling the house phone to ask to speak to your friend, or "calling" for them at their door, "You allowed out to play?"

The technology revolution has changed childhood. We may not like it but we have to accept it. We also need to understand more about how the digital lives of our children have changed their development and how they affect children's experiences. We need to do this with kindness and compassion. Every child in school should feel that they have a champion who demonstrates Unconditional Positive Regard and is able to challenge and support in equal measure. "Connection before correction" has become a term used continually in relational and trauma-informed strategy, and it forms the basis of school success. When children feel they are liked and wanted, when they feel like an adult "sees" them and is on their side, they are much more likely to want to be in school. Some children will go to school for this reason alone, because they do not have such connections in their home life.

Final thoughts

The child views reported in this chapter are from those who have been rejected from the mainstream school environment, which paints a bleak view and is representative of those who have been marginalised. It is important to acknowledge that this is not representative of all children. However, we absolutely have to work towards a future in which no child fails to fit into the education system. Sometimes referred to as our "square pegs", many of these children have individual needs that have not been met. The attendance crisis should be evidence enough that we must change what we are doing in schools. When you really think about it, it is a bizarre notion that a child would not want to attend school. The attendance crisis is sending a clear message: we aren't getting it right.

Key takeaways

1. Barriers to school attendance are complex and multi-faceted. The chapter highlights a wide range of predisposing, precipitating, and maintaining factors contributing to school attendance issues, including SEND needs, family circumstances, poor school belonging, academic pressures, and mental health challenges (House of Commons Library, 2025; DfE, 2024).
2. Children's voices emphasise mental health and unmet needs. Survey data from 218 children revealed that emotional distress, unmet SEND needs, bullying, trauma, and inflexible school environments are major drivers of school avoidance. Many families resort to home education or EOTAS after being failed by the system (Tobias, 2022; Square Peg, 2023).
3. Relational approaches and early intervention show promise. The ATTEND framework developed by Dr Tobias offers a non-blaming, collaborative approach for schools and families to identify and address barriers to attendance through joint action planning. The Nottingham MIAT model also shows success through home-based, consent-led mental health support (Hart and Heaver, 2015; Tobias, 2022).

References

Department for Education (DfE), 2023. *Permanent and Fixed Period Exclusions in England 2021/22*. London: DfE.

Department for Education (DfE), 2024. *Working Together to Improve School Attendance: Guidance for Schools, Academies, Local Authorities and Governing Bodies*. London: DfE.

Education Act 1996, Section 19, 1996. *Arrangements for Education of Children Unable to Attend School for Health Reasons*. London: HMSO.

Hart, A. and Heaver, B., 2015. *Resilient Therapy: Working with Children and Families*. London: Routledge.

House of Commons Library, 2025. *School Attendance Statistics: 2022/23 and 2024/25 Estimates*. London: UK Parliament.

Maxwell Martin, A., 2024. BBC Radio 4 interview on school attendance and mental health. BBC Sounds [broadcast].

Office for National Statistics (ONS), 2023. *Pupil Absence in Schools in England: Autumn and Spring Terms 2022/23*. London: ONS.

Roffey, S., 2012. *Pupil Well-Being and Behaviour in School*. Maidenhead: Open University Press.

Square Peg, 2023. Not Fine in School: Parent advocacy and school avoidance. Available at: https://www.notfineinschool.co.uk.

Tobias, A., 2022. ATTEND framework: Supporting emotionally based school avoidance. Brighton and Hove Educational Psychology Service.

7

Attendance, the LA, and the wider system

Jennifer Hardy

The previous chapter reported the growing number of children with mental health issues in our schools and the barriers that prevent them from going to school. For local authorities (LAs), children not attending due to their mental health is one of an emerging number of pressures piled onto an already challenging education landscape. Currently riding high in the charts alongside the mental health challenges of our young people, we have the rapidly increasing numbers of children with complex special educational needs and disabilities (SEND); budgets that cannot keep up with this level of growth; a surge in children being removed from school rolls to be home educated; and an increase in permanent exclusion.

LAs are a key stakeholder in the education system and have many statutory responsibilities in supporting children with their mental health, but with no influence over how these young people are first supported in schools. While we cannot shape the offer for young people when they are in school, unless we want to pick up all of the pieces when they stop attending completely, we must develop and rely on our relationships with our schools, settings, and multi-academy trusts (MATs) to work together at every step of the graduated response.

For LAs, the Department for Education's (DfE) *Working Together to Improve School Attendance* guidance, which became statutory on the last day of August in 2024, is incredibly clear about how young people should be supported in school if they cannot attend for any health reason, and when the LA should become involved. The document champions the requirement for schools to "develop and maintain a whole school culture that promotes the benefits of high attendance" and advises schools to "recognise absence is a symptom and that improving pupil's attendance is part of improving the pupil's overall welfare". But how easy is this to achieve across a whole school with competing demands, pressures, and the day-to-day issues all schools face?

The guidance assigns responsibility to the LA for supporting pupils to overcome barriers to attendance and facilitate the wider support children and their families need that will help a child to come to school. The LA's key responsibilities are:

1. Track local attendance data – now much easier thanks to the DfE's Wonde attendance recording system
2. Have a school attendance team, usually known as an Education Welfare Service, which provides these key functions:
    a. Communication, training, and advice
    b. Targeting support meetings with schools
    c. Multi-disciplinary support for families
    d. Legal intervention

Increasingly, these teams will be supporting families and schools where a child's mental health concerns have become so significant the child is no longer attending school and, like everyone else in the system, they are having to pivot the support they offer and increase their knowledge to navigate this field. A good service will develop their offer in conjunction with the schools and settings under their remit and will ensure it reflects the needs of their population.

However, it's the targeting support meetings that give LAs the opportunity for those regular conversations with schools about individual, whole school strategies, and support for improving their attendance. These meetings, and the information gathered in them, highlight the vast difference between schools in the way they ensure a whole school approach to improving attendance.

In relation to supporting children with their mental health, conversations with schools reveal the depths most education professionals go to for their young people, and the passion, ambition, and care they have. Many schools are creating specific physical spaces to support children with their mental health needs, and these "bridge" type provisions aim to allow children to still attend school without the physical challenges being in the main building brings.

One school I know that does this really well is blessed with a smaller building between the main gates into school and the main school building. They have established a base here for their emotional-based school avoiders. Pupils come to school, normally after the main school has started, and they still access the school site but come straight to this building where they have a softer start to the day and receive a bespoke curriculum. From here, they will be supported to access the main school part-time, building up incrementally until they no longer require the use of the smaller base.

Not all schools will have this type of provision, and if they do have spare space, the demands on it are probably significant, but having an on-site base specifically for these children can be really beneficial, and relying on ever-evolving technology to try to keep people immersed in their actual classrooms is a brilliant tool.

The targeting support team meetings can also reveal some missed opportunities when it comes to engaging or re-engaging a child with mental health challenges, and these predominantly relate to schools that have not yet managed to embed a whole school approach to school attendance.

Attendance leads must be part of the senior leadership team (SLT), and teams must be integrated

Some schools have identified school attendance officers and leads who work in isolation to other teams in their school, such as SEND teams, pastoral leads, and year group leaders. This leaves them unable to pull together a whole picture of a child and their barriers to attendance, and also means they can't support or challenge parents when the child stops attending.

There can also be challenges when schools do not have their attendance as a specific part of the role of someone on an SLT. Without having a seat at the table for key strategic meetings, discussions, and decisions, school attendance leads are in the dark about the impact of school policies on attendance and how changes in provision, funding, timetabling, etc. will impact the children they are trying the hardest to support.

An example I have of the above was during a visit where I shadowed our Education Welfare Team. We met with the attendance team for a busy secondary school. We discussed the cases all parties were most concerned about, and it soon became evident that all of the children being discussed had additional needs. However, the attendance team had very little knowledge of SEND and any of the possible reasonable adjustments that could be offered for these children to reflect their needs. It seemed their job was to hound parents every day for not sending their children to school, but they could do very little to entice them back in.

Communication needs to be really clear at all levels

Developing a whole school approach to improving school attendance is no mean feat and is something that will happen incrementally. Clear, consistent communication and regular information sharing are really key, and this is an area we often see causes a problem between schools and parents. For children who are anxious about coming to school, reasonable adjustments are recommended regularly by the DfE, and these can be as simple as a delayed start to the day, uniform adjustments, safe space to eat lunch, and so on. Whilst the adjustments themselves are simple, having them widely communicated to the many people who come into contact with the child during the school day is very challenging, and too often this seemingly simple step can cause further disruption to engagement from children already struggling to engage with school.

I am aware of a case where a child had stopped attending school entirely and one of their perceived challenges was in relation to some children in their form class. As a mitigation, and to re-engage the child, they were promised a move to a different classroom when they returned to school by the senior member of staff supporting their attendance improvement plan. It took a lot for this child to come back into school, for them and for their family, and on the day they returned they came in later as agreed, were greeted by the receptionist, and then immediately escorted to their old form room with the same children they had been asked to be moved from.

Now while this is a simple mistake that could be easily rectified, the impact of this communication lapse on the child and their family was so significant in eroding trust and increasing school-based anxiety that the child has yet to return to mainstream education. This is an unusual example, but the feedback we gather from discussions with parents and schools often cites a communication breakdown as one of the reasons for children not attending school.

Whole school means *whole school*

If you have ever been fortunate enough to see Wayne Harris deliver his training about Inclusive Attendance, as outlined in Chapter 6 you will be familiar with his challenge for every level of school staff to be responsible for improving school attendance. In 2023, Maddi Popoola and I interviewed children who were on roll with the hospital school in the area to ask about their experiences in mainstream education and their journey to a place at the hospital school, and one of the most interesting pieces of feedback they provided was about their experiences at lunch time, which really echoed Wayne's sentiments.

The children talked about how they felt pressure at lunch time from a really young age and how this contributed to their experiences in mainstream school. Being forced to finish their dinner or eat a certain amount of it before they could leave the table was regularly brought up, as well as the replacement of their usual teachers with lunch time staff, both of which caused them challenges when they were in primary school. Now I am not against teachers having a lunch break, but a whole school culture really does need to mean the whole school, so these staff need to be part of in-service education and training (INSET) day briefings, and information sharing whenever possible.

When these children entered secondary school, the main issues they faced were bullying, friendship group challenges, a lack of quiet spaces for them to go to, and, for one child, being tracked by a member of staff using a pair of binoculars when they were out on the playground or field "for their own safety".

The case studies above are meant to support education professionals to identify some of the nuanced changes that could be made in their own settings, and it hopefully goes without saying that the vast majority of schools and school staff strive to deliver their very best for their pupils and their families. That being said, when it comes to supporting children with their mental health issues, even that sometimes doesn't work, and these children often end up the responsibility of the LA because they become home educated or they qualify as children under the Section 19 pathway, which means they have been unable to attend school for 15 days or more due to physical or mental health challenges. The Section 19 guidance places the LA with the responsibility of educating all Section 19 children.

Elective home education

As I said at the start of this chapter, elective home education (EHE) is one of the growing areas of pressure experienced by LAs and the wider system. It is also an example where government policy about LAs' lack of ability to influence practice in schools is matched by the fact we become responsible for these children when they can no longer cope with their school situation.

LAs must report termly on their EHE figures in the DfE's Children Missing Education return. In Autumn 2024, 111,700 children were reported to be home educated in England. This was an increase from 92,000 in Autumn 2023.

Other than a parent's philosophical views about education, a child's mental health was the highest reason given for becoming EHE in 2023/2024 and the autumn term of 2024/2025, with an average of 14% across all of the termly returns.

Whilst the removal of a child with mental health concerns from the rigour of school may bring some immediate relief and reduction in pressure placed on them, there *could* be, based on the child's home situation, significant risks for the child and their family if the protective factor of school is no longer there to support them. Recent changes to the DfE's guidance for EHE have increased this risk significantly. Previously, when a parent indicated they were considering EHE, the LA would be part of a three-way meeting with school and the family to understand the reasons for considering EHE and identify whether this was really what the child and parent wanted or if it was a request for more support. The ability to hold this meeting was recently removed by updated guidance from the DfE, which says schools should remove a child from roll upon receipt of communication from the parent that states they wish to move to EHE.

They are, not just metaphorically, voting with their feet. In Nottingham, we've had to create a whole new category for these children. We call them EHEE – elective home educated enquiries. They have indicated a desire to be home educated, so they are no longer on roll at school, but until we can be satisfied there is a plan to actually educate them at home, they remain in this enquiry stage. And there can be hundreds of them.

For some children and families, being home educated is the right thing to do and it can bring joy, balance, and a new way of life to those who need it. But so many parents and children are finding themselves on this EHE pathway because their child's mental health needs mean they can no longer cope with school and, sometimes, the parent's mental health also is a barrier.

Final thoughts

The answer, for me, is to go right back to the beginning to when a child's mental health began to be a barrier to them attending school regularly, properly unpick the reasons for this, put in place some of the many easy-to-implement reasonable adjustments, continue to review their progress, and support the child and their family to thrive at school. This book outlines the reasons school needs to change, and provides a wealth of suggestions and examples of how we can make schools a better place to be for *all* children. School should be a place of refuge and kindness, where all children want to be, not "forced" by departmental legislation. When a child goes down the EHE path as a result of no longer being able to cope in school or because the parents can no longer take the challenge about their school attendance, it is too late; the support and safety measures of being in school are removed, and trying to get back into that environment becomes much harder.

Key takeaways

1. Local authorities (LAs) face increasing pressures around attendance and special educational needs and disabilities (SEND). LAs are dealing with growing numbers of children with complex SEND needs, mental health difficulties, and rising cases of elective home education (EHE) linked to school anxiety. They have statutory duties to track attendance and support families, but limited influence over early school-based interventions (Butler et al., 2025; DfE, 2024a).
2. Whole school, collaborative approaches are critical but inconsistent. The chapter stresses the importance of integrating school attendance leads into senior leadership and fostering communication between attendance, SEND, and pastoral teams. Poor communication and failure to embed reasonable adjustments can severely erode trust and lead to further disengagement from education.

3. The rise in elective home education is a growing concern. The number of children reported as home educated rose from 92,000 (2023) to 111,700 (2024), with mental health being the second most cited reason after philosophical beliefs. The removal of LA involvement in pre-EHE decision-making has raised safeguarding risks for vulnerable children (DfE, 2024b).

References

Butler, P., Duncan, P., Pearce, M., and Boyd, R., 2025, 30 March. Nearly 20 councils in England "at risk of insolvency" due to SEND costs. *The Guardian*.

Department for Education (DfE), 2024a. *Working Together to Improve School Attendance: Guidance for Schools, Academies, Local Authorities and Governing Bodies*. London: DfE.

Department for Education (DfE), 2024b. *Arranging Education for Children Unable to Attend School Due to Health Needs*. London: DfE.

8

The Covid legacy
What has been lost, missed, and gained?
Sarah Sivers

> *I am worried about catching up with my school work.*
> Child

Introduction

There is a conversation that needs to be had about the legacy of Covid-19, which goes beyond the academic factors discussed in the previous chapter and focuses on wider experiences – developmental, social, and emotional. As Educational Psychologists we are mapping the developmental legacy of Covid-19 in almost every conversation we have about children and young people.

The experience of living through a global pandemic that changed the way we live needs to be considered, to understand how children, young people, and adults manage the world around them. There is a usefulness and benefit in counting back to see the age the child or young person was at the time of the pandemic, and what skills they might have been developing at that time. This can be seen in terms of exploring individual development, what was missed or gained from the changes in life and education brought about by lockdown restrictions. There are also patterns across groups to be considered in terms of social skills, managing and understanding emotions, attention, and concentration, all of which can be understood in terms of experiences that were missed or gained during Covid-19.

This chapter will also consider the positive aspects and the gains that many children and young people experienced during Covid-19, and we can also think about how we can offer children and young people the time, space, and opportunity to practise skills they may not have had the opportunity to practise at a younger age. We also want to look ahead and think about the future in a hopeful way: what are the things we can focus on, adapt, change, keep, and build?

However, while it is important to look at what was lost, missed, or gained as a result of the pandemic, we also need to look at what was happening before Covid-19 to really understand context, influence, and impact. The world is constantly changing. So much change occurred before Covid-19 that affected the way we experienced it (i.e. technological advances), and so much has happened in the five years since. It is important to reflect on what happened before, during, and after, and to embrace change, look for opportunities, and contemplate what might be and what is. This is what we aim to do in this chapter.

Reflection

This book is grounded in the research we carried out over four years to hear, understand, and share the experiences and views of children and young people as they lived through the Covid-19 pandemic. The fundamental aim of this research has been to gain the views of the children and young people, to truly hear what they had to say, and to do something with that information. There was also a strong desire to offer a different voice to that being shared through the media at the time of the pandemic and as we moved away from it. We still feel that this is a topic that needs to be explored and understood, a conversation that needs to be had. This is why you have this book in your hand!

On a very general level, the Covid-19 pandemic changed the way we all think and the language we use. What was your understanding and use of the word "pandemic" before March 2020? It was a word maybe more associated with a history lesson, now a lived experience. We talked of lockdown and shielding, coronavirus and Covid-19, bubbles and "the 2-metre rule". There was also a popular metaphor stated at the time: we were in the same storm, but in different boats – a creative use of language to make sense of what we were experiencing then. However, we were in those boats before the pandemic; Covid-19 was just a new storm to manage and navigate. There were many things that were working and not working within education before the pandemic, and many of these things persist today.

The pandemic created change in large and small ways, which we are only just starting to understand now as we write this book in 2025. The important thing to keep in mind is the need to stop and reflect; to think about what happened and what might be different now. We don't often take the time to really reflect on the things that happen to us. We invite you to do that now before we dive into this chapter on legacy.

Reflection point

A few questions for you:

- *What do you remember most about the pandemic? What was the first thing that popped into your mind? What has stayed with you? Is it a particular experience you went through? An overall emotion? A place or thing?*
- *Have you actually taken time to really think about what that time gave you, took away from you, or offered you?*

The issue is that thinking about the pandemic and its effects (positive and negative) has drifted away; it is no longer good copy or clickbait. However, the pandemic is still causing ripples, and this chapter will consider these ripples in relation to children and young people's development, plus their engagement with and experience of school and learning. We will explore these ripples using psychological frameworks to guide us, and consider the research that is being carried out to understand the legacy of Covid-19.

Systemic layers of influence and impact

The bioecological or process–person–context–time (PPCT) model (Bronfenbrenner, 1999; Bronfenbrenner and Morris, 1998, 2006) offers a useful framework to consider the influence and impact of Covid-19. This model allows us to consider the bi-directional influence and impact of interactions between an individual and different aspects of their environment. Returning to the metaphor of different boats in the same sea offers us a way to make sense of this model.

An individual person in a particular boat will have their own unique skills, knowledge, and experience; the other people in that boat will influence that

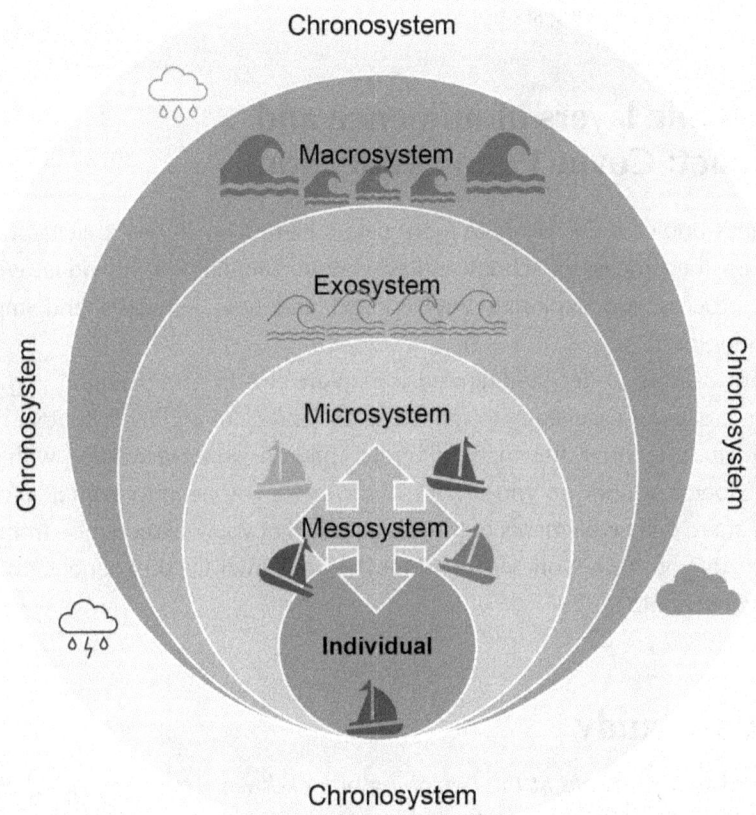

Figure 8.1 Bioecological model

experience and be influenced by the individual. However, the construction of the boat, how it is navigated, the place in which it is situated in the sea, and what is around provide a context that will have an influence and impact. This again is bi-directional as this boat can affect what is going on for the individual, others in the boat, and those on other boats. The wider sea and those who may have control over who goes where or does what is a further layer of context to understand influence and impact, as does the time when this is all occurring and historical factors. The weather can represent historical events over time, which shift and change, never staying the same – just like the weather.

Figure 8.1 is an attempt to make visual sense of these systemic influences and impacts and the multi-dimensional interactions that occur. It also introduces the names given by Bronfenbrenner (1977) for the various systems or contexts within which development occurs. These will be explored in more depth in the following section.

Systemic layers of influence and impact: Covid-19 and education

So let's unpick these layers in more detail. Here we will be explicitly focusing on the process of school and education, situating an individual within this process and exploring how context and time influence and impact development.

For ease of understanding and to explore this in a meaningful way, we have created a case study to introduce an individual and their context. This case study incorporates many different children we have worked with and is deliberately open so you can make the sense you need to from it. We are sure there will be elements of this case study that you will recognise from the contexts you have worked in and maybe your own lived experience of life and/or school.

Case study

S was 5 years old at the beginning of lockdown. They live with their Mum, Dad, and two siblings, M (10 years old) and L (2 years old). S's parents both work long shifts in retail and hospitality professions. S's younger sibling, L, has health needs. S's extended family live in a different country.

The family live in a small town which has seen local businesses and traditional industries close; there is a high level of unemployment. The local environment requires modernisation and there are limited open spaces for people to spend time in. There are community concerns around drugs and county lines influences. The schools the children attend are currently graded by Ofsted as Good (Primary School) and Requiring Improvement (Secondary School).

We will now consider S, their family, and environment through the lens of the bioecological model. We will start with focusing on experiences at the time of the pandemic (2020–2021) and then go on to consider how these experiences may have influenced S's subsequent development and that of their siblings.

Chronosystem (2020–2021)

The chronosystem represents wider historical and cultural events that have an impact on the way life is lived or thought about. This also applies to individual transitions in life such as starting or changing school or a job, and moving house or country.

Wider: the Covid-19 pandemic led to lockdown measures being put in place across the UK from March 2020. There were a number of national and local lockdowns that continued until July 2021. People were asked to stay at home, many workplaces were closed, and only vulnerable children and those from key worker families attended school.

There were incidents of national local unrest based on inequalities and discrimination, which resulted in demonstrations and riots.

Austerity and the cost-of-living crisis had an impact.

Technological changes gained pace, with the internet becoming a part of everyday life.

Microsystems

Microsystems encompass the interactions between an individual (in this case S) and those they have direct contact with (family, school, friends, etc.). This relationship is bi-directional.

Family system: circumstances were difficult financially and emotionally, which caused stress. Both parents were at home as their places of work were closed.

They were not able to return to work until the end of lockdown as the family needed to shield to protect the health of the youngest child, which caused high anxiety in the family.

Connection with extended family and friends was through phone calls. They were not able to visit for many years due to travel restrictions.

S's parents attempted to home school the children, but S did not want to do school work at home and became frustrated. This influenced S's parents' confidence in being able to educate their children.

The family enjoyed engaging in cooking and art activities together.

School system: S had some contact with their reception teacher and a friend through phone calls.

S returned to school in September 2020 and joined a small class bubble with adults and children they did not know well.

S experienced bullying from one child within their bubble, which impacted on the way they interacted with their siblings at home.

S found it hard to settle back to school.

Community system: the family were not able to engage in community groups and activities as these had all been cancelled. This created a sense of isolation and reduced the support network available to the family.

Mesosystem

The interconnection and interaction between an individual's microsystems, in S and their siblings' case the family, school, peer group, and community.

Family and school systems: the family system (S's parents) and the school system (teachers) did communicate. School provided the family with IT resources to support engagement with learning and offered motivating activities to engage S and support their parents. This offered a supportive and collaborative approach to helping S engage with learning and settle back into school.

However, the interaction between the school system and family system in relation to M was very different, with differences of opinion in terms of "catch-up learning" and zero tolerance approaches in the new secondary school. This resulted in a breakdown in relationships and a reduction in M's attendance.

School and peer group systems: the interactions that occurred between the school system and peer group in relation to consequences for unkindness did not address the support the children needed. This resulted in continued conflict and had an impact on S's self-esteem and sense of belonging in school.

M's experience of feeling unsettled and unsupported in their new school led to them seeking out a new peer group outside school to gain a sense of belonging. This peer group reinforced the negative view M was developing of school and school became more punitive because of M's connection with this group.

Exosystem

Formal and informal systems that have an indirect impact on an individual, in this case the influence government policies and media coverage of Covid-19, education, or work policies had on S, their family, and school.

Family system: the media coverage around illness and death were incredibly emotive and anxiety-provoking as there was a family member with health conditions. The new narratives around shielding and isolation permeated the family and changed their interactions with the local community. The restrictions put in place during the Covid-19 lockdown meant the professions in which S's parents worked were shut down for an extended period and then subject to restrictions when re-opened. This impacted on the family financially and emotionally.

School system: the narrative around lost learning and the need for catch-up had an influence on the way school framed learning and attainment. The secondary school M started at in September 2020 focused on "lost learning", which was different to the family's focus on wellbeing.

Macrosystem

The wider cultural ideologies, attitudes, and structures within the society in which an individual exists, in this case the established norms and values that influence the systems around S.

Community system: norms and values shifted and changed. There were fights over toilet rolls and people became wary of being in proximity to other people. There was a watchfulness and fear; this was sometimes counterbalanced by a shared experience, such as clapping for the NHS.

Family system: the social structures and attitudes around race, class, and culture had an impact on S's family and their sense of belonging and safety in the community; and the value placed on community, relationships, education, belonging, inclusion, and how the community was being supported to develop and thrive. This influenced the experiences of the family microsystem in their day-to-day working life.

School system: the dominant narrative around the importance of academic learning and the need for academic qualifications or a certain level of learning to be successful influenced the approach of the school microsystem. Added to this is the ideology around discipline in school, such as zero tolerance and the way this influences how schools manage learning relationships.

This exploration of experience using the bioecological model can be read either way to understand the interconnecting interactions of each system with the individual and again how that might be changed by the way an individual, group, or system responds. Nothing happens in a vacuum; we live in a dynamic world and that world changes and shifts in small and large ways every day. Let us now look at what has happened since Covid-19 and how sense is being made of these changes.

What do we know about the impact of Covid-19: What has changed and what was already there?

The above example provided a view into how Covid-19 influenced people's lives, but also acknowledged that it was not a phenomenon that existed alone. The pandemic occurred within a certain period of time, alongside other events. In some ways it was a perfect storm with such a combination of difficult circumstances coming around the same point. However, there is value in looking at the impact of Covid-19 as a novel and unique event.

A sense of feeling safe in the world

We wanted to pick up here on the concept of safety as it permeated through the example we have just given – safety in the face of Covid-19, financial safety, emotional safety at school, feeling safe in the community we live in. This is something that threaded through all of the research we have conducted and we feel needs a particular mention because of the profound nature of feeling safe.

One of the unique impacts of Covid-19 is how it has shifted people's sense of safety. The worst did happen in terms of illness and death, and this has left a legacy for most people. There was always a slight sense of distaste if someone sneezed or coughed near you, but this is now tinged with something different. The idea of being in a crowded space may conjure different feelings now. The children and young people who responded to our surveys spoke of being concerned that they would take "the virus" home and family members "might die". There was talk of bubbles and isolating, changing the meaning of everyday language. There will be a generation of children and adults where the song "Happy Birthday" will bring memories of washing their hands, as well as cake and presents!

Imagine being S, a 5-year-old child whose world is turned upside down because of a virus that not only changes their daily life but also causes a real risk to a member of their family. Their school says stay at home, their parents' work says stay at home, and the TV gives a constant stream of "wash your hands" while delivering the numbers of people who have died. This makes the world a very scary and unsafe place. This is a place you are only just beginning to make sense of, a place you have just begun to step into more independently in starting school, and then suddenly it is a place of danger.

Imagine being a child who does not have a settled family experience, and as well as growing up with an external world that is uncertain and frightening, this is also your experience in your microsystem. You may be exposed to violence, drug-taking, and neglect; during Covid-19 you would have been at home more, without the additional watchful safeguarding eye of others in the school, community, wider family, etc. These experiences would affect how you approach and manage the world around you, likely bringing disadvantages and difficulties. This would have been the experience anyway, but it is now exacerbated by Covid-19.

Then there are all the other experiences between the two outlined above, all the different boats floating around. We have heard stories of children and young people who had been finding it incredibly difficult to attend school before Covid-19, but then found it easier to return to school afterwards because there was less focus on them, as so many other people were also returning. There were the children and young people who had been perceived to be doing fine, but were actually masking all the difficulties they were experiencing. The chance to be at home made them realise that there was a different way; these are the children and young people who found it hard to return or who didn't return at all.

Those formative experiences, at such a young age, in such an intense, all-consuming and ever-present manner, do not easily disappear. This is the legacy of Covid-19 on the children and young people who had little or no conscious awareness of life before the pandemic and those who knew and understood exactly what was going on. This is not an experience that can be put down and forgotten about; there is a lasting quality to this experience, and this is what we are seeing in the schools and classrooms across the UK and across the world. It has also changed the way in which people view school and education, as well as its importance and purpose.

There are some narratives and thoughts around Covid-19 that have persisted to some extent or are returned to when the media or politicians feel the need to. We will consider these in more detail below.

Crisis?

The idea of a crisis takes us back to the power of the media and the dominant narratives that are accorded prominence at any given time. At the time of Covid-19 and for a while afterwards there was a huge focus on "lost learning" and "the mental health crisis" as if they were a direct effect of the pandemic. This narrative led to time, focus, and money being placed on "catch-up" programmes and advice around mental health; some of this was well-meaning, some aspects helpful, but rarely was it acknowledged that these things already existed separate from Covid-19.

Those of us working in education already knew there were multifaceted issues within education, and wider attitudes and structures around learning, development, and mental health. This wasn't a crisis as much as a way of life with academic, socio-economic, cultural gaps and real problems in accessing resources for those who were on the wrong side of this gap. What needed to be amplified was not a story of a crisis that was emerging, but how to really understand and make sense of what was going wrong through the additional lens of Covid-19. There was and still is the invitation to take what happened as an opportunity for change and reflection, a chance to recalibrate as we suggested in the reports, chapter, and journal articles we created from the pupil views work (i.e. Popoola and Sivers, 2021; Popoola and Sivers, 2023).

There was research and thinking at the time of the pandemic that predicted the potential impact, and much of it was negative. But much of it was focused on more tangible factors such as language, learning, social, and emotional (considered below). However, the more profound impacts, such as basic needs and a sense of safety, underpin those tangible factors. These are the bottom layers of Maslow's Hierarchy of Needs (1954); and feeling safe is fundamental.

The "catch-up" learning narrative seems to have receded slightly, and while it does re-emerge at certain times (exam results day), there seems to be less media interest in this idea. I wonder why. There is still much we have to learn from the impact of Covid-19 and the effect it has had on children's development; not so much the recall of facts and figures, which was the focus on the catch-up narrative, but much more profound skills than are the usual focus in the current education system.

These skills include attention, social interaction skills, motivation, confidence, and perseverance. These are skills that would have been learned in the day-to-day hustle and bustle of family life, or at nursery, or at the park. Many children missed out on experiences that we knew were important, but now we are seeing quite how important and on a larger scale than we have seen before. The conversations we are having with teaching staff and parents give insights into the impact missing early socialisation in nursery or just out and about has had on children's confidence; and the impact of spending time in a small family bubble with fewer opportunities for having to share attention or wait is having on attention and focus in the classroom.

Is it right to name these experiences a crisis? Some of the children would have had differences and difficulties, in their learning, mental health, and experiences of the world, regardless of Covid-19; but some of these differences have been exacerbated by Covid-19. Some children may have just got by, flown under the radar, but are seen now because those skills that could have seen them through are not there. Some children would have been fine and on the whole still are fine, most of the time; but they still experience a degree of worry and uncertainty that may not have been there before the pandemic.

Academic learning and mental health are topics that we cover through this book. Here it is enough to acknowledge that these areas have been around for many years. There have been significant changes in education and how it is viewed and delivered, e.g. how we view additional needs and how this is supported in school (the introduction of the SEN Code of Practice in 1994 and subsequent updates). The first statutory National Curriculum was introduced in 1988, but it has undergone many changes and is under review again as we write in 2025, with an interim report just published. There have been extensive changes and shifts in how we view and think about mental health and emotional wellbeing across all age ranges. These areas will always need revising and reviewing as we need to respond to changes in life and experience, which includes the influence and impact of Covid-19; life does not stand still. However, what is frustrating is that the same themes recur because they are not addressed adequately. This includes the four areas suggested for further focus in the just published Curriculum Review (Review Panel, 2025), which are the need to: address the socio-economic attainment gap, create a more diverse curriculum, respond to social and technological change, and review post 16 pathways. These are not new issues! They were there long before Covid-19.

While in this book we share the experiences children and young people had during Covid-19, it is important not to see the pandemic as a static baseline with which to explore, analyse, or predict change. It needs to be viewed as one of many punctuation marks, which can be used to make sense of this ever-changing life we live. However, alongside technological changes such as the internet, it is a very important punctuation mark and one that needs to be threaded through our understanding and planning for education (and life). Its legacy needs to be as an event we can look before and beyond to add to our knowledge.

An example of this can be seen in a scoping literature review conducted by Zuniga-Montanez et al. (2025) to explore the impact Covid-19 had on language development. They found that there was a consistent theme of decline in language development across the literature reviewed, including social communication, vocabulary, plus aspects such as readiness for school, academic language, and progress. They also found that this impact was apparent across many countries and all socio-economic contexts. However, there was a disproportionate impact on families from impoverished socio-economic backgrounds, and Covid-19 exacerbated inequalities that already existed. In addition, one of the factors that was suggested to influence a decline in language development was increased use of technology; this could only have been a factor as a result of technological advances and accessibility. This one example shows that the interplay before, during, and after needs to be considered to even begin to understand change, influence, and impact of events.

There are many areas of change and much we still need to explore as time moves on. What will the long-term gains and losses be? Our research and that of many others have provided real insight into the gains and losses the children and young people experienced in the moment, and then how this influenced their experiences in the short and medium term. We need to keep reflecting on the patterns that are emerging and think about what the impact might be in the long term; the ripples that continue to fan out. That is why we will now return to the bioecological model to explore how we might look to the future with some plans and hope.

Systemic layers of influence and impact: Looking to the future with hope

Let's flip the coin and see things from *now* and look forward with some hope. We will take the same systems but focus instead on change and development that could happen and the influence and impact this could have. This will be a broad sweep of ideas, which will be expanded upon in the final chapter of this book where we look at next steps and ideas in more depth.

We will still start with the chronosystem, but we will take a top-down view this time to look at how the different systems might influence positive change in general and for S and their family.

Chronosystem

Covid-19 and other events that have occurred in the last five years have energised many to think, "if not now, when?" This question is asked here in terms of education in particular. There are many voices speaking for changes in approach, focus, and content of education. Education is currently in a state of flux. Consider how many Education Secretaries we have had since 2020 There is much to reflect on in terms of the time we are in and if we are taking advantage of the positive aspects that came from Covid-19. We are in a time where we are learning the impact of Covid-19 (as considered here), and this research and learning need to continue. We need to understand the ripples of developmental changes we are seeing in early years settings, classrooms, and workplaces across the country (and across the world).

We are in a time where information technology and the "meta universe" evolves so quickly but is so little understood. We have more of an awareness of Mental Health on a surface level, but there is so much work to do to change dominant narratives and develop understanding. We are in a time of fake news and drama, but how can we counterbalance that noise?

Macrosystem

How can we shift cultural norms and expectations to be more inclusive, affirming, and appreciative of difference? This is a huge shift, but like turning our ship, it starts with a small turn of the wheel. This book and many others like it that are being published every day are the small turn of the wheel. Every teacher, parent, governor, councillor, blogger, politician, or journalist who picks up these ideas and shares them in a useful and proactive way helps the wheel turn. This whole book espouses approaches based on trauma-informed thinking, and these are the narratives we feel need to inform policy makers in education (plus health and social care). We need to ground policies and practices in a narrative of belonging, safety, and hope.

We also need higher expectations of education, for the content and approach to be grounded in diversity and offer a rich, decolonised curriculum that offers skills appropriate for the 21st century learners we mentioned in other chapters, plus motivation for life-long engagement with learning and growth.

Exosystem

The wider narratives suggested above will then trickle down into the day-to-day life of school. Imagine that the relational approaches we espoused in Chapter 4 replaced zero tolerance in every school. Imagine that children and young people, teaching staff, and parents felt truly part of a school community that welcomed their unique contributions. Imagine that we took some of the things that worked in Covid-19 and made them standard – hybrid learning approaches that allowed the many children and young people with health needs (physical and mental) to access learning all the time; technology and affordable Wi-Fi provided to all families in socio-economic impoverishment so they have resources with which to learn (the majority of information, homework, and resources are accessed via online portals).

We need our schools to be allowed to embrace innovative ways to educate and to move away from a purely academic focus, which disadvantages so many children and young people. As we have seen in other chapters, the future workforces require skills in problem-solving, leadership, resilience, and empathy. This will not be developed through equations and Shakespeare alone; although teaching these things well and with enthusiasm could be achieved.

Mesosystem

One of the key factors in the hopeful exosystem outlined above is that children, young people, teaching staff, and families truly feel part of a community.

This will foster interconnection and connectedness within the mesosystem. Even if there are times of conflict, the ideas around relational approaches and cooperation will support these difficult times and enable space to work through them. There might even be space for an acknowledgement that this environment, this mix of people, this approach is not working for everyone involved and so try something different. Let's go back to our idea that there is no one size fits all approach. There are square pegs, round pegs, triangular pegs; and all shapes and sizes of pegs and holes need to be adapted to fit each one. (This makes a change from the boat metaphor!)

Microsystem

If the outside world is more welcoming, inclusive, and supportive, then the individual and those closest to them will have more capacity to manage tricky times and mourn losses together, and there will be the space to enjoy life and to manage any ruptures and repair with understanding, with space to build resilience together and celebrate the gains. This will help develop children and young people who feel they matter and can have a positive impact on the people around them. This then ripples out to the experiences they have across life and environments. These experiences will not be without challenges and times of difficulty, but the skills and resources will be there to be used and shared.

Who benefits from these ideas? Everyone!

Final thoughts

In this chapter we have reflected on the legacy of Covid-19 and suggested that, in relation to education, this legacy needs to be seen as part of a wider timeframe of change and a wider system of narratives, attitudes, and structures. Covid-19 needs to be seen as a (very important) punctuation point. We need to take in what was happening before (the so-called crises in education and mental health did not start with Covid-19) and what happened during the pandemic itself (what worked and what didn't). Finally, we need to understand the legacy from different viewpoints to gain a truly layered understanding of what happened in all the boats that sailed into Covid-19, sailed through it, and came out the other side. We need to consider the losses, difficulties, changes, and joy, and we need to think about what we keep and what we let go. We need to remember and move forward with hope.

What this chapter has highlighted is that life is a complicated, multi-layered experience with many systems and influences acting in many directions. However, we can be active within these systems from the individual micro level to the wider macro; and we can make a difference, even if it is small. Ideas and actions can ripple, and boats can set a new course!

Key takeaways

1. The ripple effects of Covid-19 are many and varied . . .
   We are just beginning to understand what impact and influence the pandemic has had on child development. It will take time to learn what was lost and also what was gained. It is important that we take the time to reflect on what happened and not just consign it to history. We need to continue observing, discussing, and learning.
2. . . . but we can't view Covid-19 in isolation.
   We need to take a systemic view to understand the many influences on child development, on the education system, on life itself. This includes being aware of historic, cultural, and societal influences. We need to look at local communities and the resources they may or may not have, and we need to understand the experiences of an individual family and child within this wider system to know what is needed. This needs to be a top-down and bottom-up viewpoint to effect meaningful change.
3. Ruptures can lead to repair and resilience.
   If managed well, in a relational way, ruptures and challenges can be repaired, and from this repair resilience grows. In relation to the focus of this book the school system is in rupture and needs repair. The resilience is already there because this is not the first time there have been challenges, and we can learn and change. Change and growth is hard and cannot be done by one person alone; but when enough people align and seek positive ways to create positive change, magic can happen.

References

Bronfenbrenner, U., 1977. Toward an experimental ecology of human development. *American Psychologist*, 32(7), pp. 513–531.

Bronfenbrenner, U., 1999. *Environments in Developmental Perspective: Theoretical and Operational Models*. Washington, DC: US Department of Health and Human Services.

Bronfenbrenner, U. and Morris, P.A., 1998. The ecology of developmental processes. In R.M. Lerner (ed.), *Handbook of Child Psychology: Theoretical Models of Human Development* (pp. 993–1028). 5th ed. New York: Wiley.

Bronfenbrenner, U. and Morris, P.A., 2006. The bioecological model of human development. In R.M. Lerner and W. Damon (Eds.), *Handbook of Child Psychology: Theoretical Models of Human Development* (pp. 793–828). 6th ed. Hoboken, NJ: John Wiley & Sons.

Maslow, A.H., 1954. *Motivation and Personality*. New York: Harper and Row.

Popoola, M. and Sivers, S., 2021. Hearing the voices of children and young people: An ecological systems analysis of individual difference and experiences during the Covid-19 lockdown. *DECP Debate*, 177, pp. 21–25.

Popoola, M. and Sivers, S., 2023. Maslow, relationships and square pegs. In F. Morgan and E. Costello (Eds.), *Square Pegs: Inclusivity, Compassion and Fitting In – A Guide for Schools* (pp. 77–88). Bancyfelin: Independent Thinking Press.

Review Panel, 2025. *Curriculum and Assessment Review: Interim Report*. London: Crown Copyright.

Zuniga-Montanez, R., Ramos-Escobar, L.A., Harrison, L.J., and Wang, M.T., 2025. The impact of the COVID-19 pandemic on early language development: A scoping literature review. *Early Child Development and Care* [forthcoming].

9

What can we do better? From the views of children and school staff

Maddi Popoola, Louise McDonagh, and Sarah Sivers

> *I think that the school should educate us about being positive, building up self-esteem and body positivity.*
> Child

> *Teach students what they will encounter in their adult life and what can get them the best jobs out there and not things like Shakespeare.*
> Child

What else?

The very fact you picked up this book, and have made it this far, means we are hopefully on the same page. We hope that not only do you have lots of food for thought to take away with you, but also some areas to go and read more about, plus some easy strategies to start implementing in your own school or classroom, or to share with colleagues who work in schools around the UK – and the world!

However, we feel it would be remiss not to spend a few moments reflecting on some of the other areas of schools and education that we have not been able to give the time they need and deserve within the confines of this book. These are the areas we feel need review and consideration, and we also suggest some reading recommendations to dig a little deeper.

Ideas of how we can do better have been a central theme of each chapter in our book of hopes for reimagining education. This, our final chapter, is dedicated solely to the ideas that have stemmed from our research with children, and what they say they would like more (or less) of in school. In Chapter 7, the most recent data set was discussed. This was taken from a survey of children who were not attending mainstream school, for a variety of reasons. The final question on the survey asked, "What are your ideas about how school could be different, and what would have made it easier for you/what would you need to be able to go back?" A plethora of comments and ideas were shared, most of which felt easy to implement, but some of which also highlighted the need for a different type of schooling from what we may consider "mainstream". The role of specialist education will always play a part in the system, because some children are just too overwhelmed with the loudness and enormity of large mainstream schools.

The key points below are an analysis of qualitative data collected from children regarding their views on what would make school better, supported by illustrative quotations from participants. Responses highlight recurring themes of the importance of emotional support, consistency, relationships, choice, and flexibility in the learning environment.

The importance of relationships. Many children emphasised the value of positive, kind, and understanding relationships with teachers. Feeling respected, listened to, and supported emerged as critical for their engagement and emotional wellbeing:

- *"Respect for and from teaching staff. Being treated as another human being."*
- *"Helpful and kind teachers also helped me."*
- *"Teachers who understood my anxiety and didn't make me speak in class."*
- *"Everything above, but most importantly, support from kind teachers was paramount and made a massive difference to me wanting to learn and engage with lessons."*

Children frequently highlighted that it was not the structure of school itself but the presence or absence of emotionally attuned adults that shaped their experiences. We therefore can't underestimate the power of human connection within schools, or indeed any environments in which it is hoped young people will thrive. This need for having a person, a psychological partner, is quite possibly the greatest need of all. We can look to psychology for the reasons why this is so important. These comments align with **attachment theory** (Bowlby, 1969), which posits that secure relationships with caregivers or trusted adults promote emotional security and social development. In educational settings, Pianta et al. (2003) emphasise that teacher–student relationships are critical to student engagement, regulation, and resilience. Children with stronger teacher relationships are more likely to demonstrate positive behaviours, higher attendance, and academic success (Bergin and Bergin, 2009). Similarly, Social relationships with peers were a central theme. For some, friendships were a protective factor; for others, the lack of social connection or experiences of bullying contributed to negative school experiences:

- *"My friends were the only good thing. Now I have none."*
- *"Having friends and feeling part of something."*
- *"Would have been good to have good friends, but they changed into bullies too easily."*

Lack of follow-through and inconsistency. Some children described broken promises and a lack of continuity in support, contributing to mistrust and disengagement:

- *"Nothing, no help just false promises and nothing delivered."*
- *"If teachers were more open to support and follow through [on] promises made, things wouldn't have escalated."*
- *"One helpful teacher and one helpful emotional support person, but this was not enough."*

This suggests a need for schools to ensure consistent implementation of support strategies and transparent communication with students.

Emotional and mental health needs. Children shared that schools often failed to recognise or respond appropriately to their mental health challenges. The impact of anxiety, stress, and being overwhelmed was mentioned repeatedly:

- *"Having the same teacher all the time helped me . . . but not all the teachers knew about my anxiety."*
- *"Support from kind teachers was paramount."*
- *"Some teachers would allow a little time out . . . others would just shout."*

These statements resonate with **Maslow's Hierarchy of Needs** (1943), which suggests that unless children feel safe, accepted, and emotionally secure, they will be unable to focus on higher-order learning. There were repeated frustrations with **punitive behaviour systems**:

- *"Teachers told me off all the time."*
- *"I was always in trouble, even when I tried."*

This reflects concerns about traditional behaviourist strategies in schools (Skinner, 1953), which focus on punishment and rewards rather than understanding. Thorsborne and Blood (2013) advocate for **restorative practices** that promote empathy, relationship-building, and mutual respect. Several children described school experiences that felt **unsafe or distressing**:

- *"I was always sent home."*
- *"Nothing helped. Teachers couldn't give a damn about child safety or mental health."*

These align with trauma-informed education frameworks (Bath, 2008; Perry, 2006), which recognise that children exposed to adversity may present behaviours linked to unmet emotional needs. Blodgett and Lanigan (2018) report improved outcomes in schools that adopt trauma-sensitive strategies, including reduced exclusion and better emotional regulation.

Promoting wellbeing – for everyone all the time

To build further on the above recommendation to focus on the emotional wellbeing and mental health of children and young people, we need to acknowledge that promoting wellbeing needs to apply to everyone all the time. The children and young people who responded to our surveys were aware of this themselves and shared thoughts about wellbeing:

- *"Mental health needs to be as important as grades."*

As with many ideas, there is focus on having a mental health day or week, which is useful for raising awareness and reducing stigma around talking about mental health. However, wellbeing needs to be thought about every day to truly have a positive impact. It is also important to frame wellbeing as a flexible and fluid state that is about growth and embracing challenges (known by psychologists as eudaimonic wellbeing). The other end of the scale to eudaimonic wellbeing is hedonic, and this unfortunately is how a lot of people view wellbeing and what they strive for or promote. Hedonic wellbeing focuses on maximising pleasure and minimising unhappiness; the drive is for a problem-free existence with no stress or distress. This is unrealistic, and seeking this "perfect" level of wellbeing can be counterproductive, because life is complicated and problems do happen. The road to wellbeing is being flexible and discovering resources that will help to manage challenges as well as celebrate achievements.

I (Sarah) have been invited to many education settings to run workshops on wellbeing with the staff. I share the hedonic and eudaimonic ideas around wellbeing presented above and we think about whether that is their way of thinking and if it is a message that is passed on to the children and young people. How can we promote the eudaimonic view of wellbeing?

I always start by telling the group I am working with that I am not there to give them a list of strategies that will automatically create wellbeing; wellbeing is unique to each individual and it takes thought and effort. What I do share is the six ways to wellbeing framework (Aked et al., 2008; Basarkod, 2019). This framework highlights the key areas that have been found to influence individual wellbeing in a positive way. See Figure 9.1.

I use this framework with the adults and young people I work with to explore what wellbeing looks like for them. What I feel is motivating about this framework is the flexibility of it: it opens you up to think about what you do, or need to do more of, to bring these areas into your life. Again, I often say to the staff and young people I work with that they have to bring these areas into their lives with joy and purpose. It will not work if they just think, "Sarah said if I do something in each area then my wellbeing will be great!" You have to find the things that work for you and bring you joy. For one person, being active will be regularly running 5km; for someone else it will be dancing round their kitchen or doing the gardening. Find your thing and do it wholeheartedly. Do it because you enjoy it and you want to do it, not because someone else has told you it will be good for you.

As already mentioned, you need to take time to reflect and find your own ways to wellbeing. Take time to reflect on what you do and don't do in each area. Ask yourself the question, "What do I do to connect with others?" and do this for each area. If there is one where you find it hard to think of anything you do, find a way to bring this into your life in some way, or support the young person to explore these areas. Check back in with what you are doing regularly; it might be helpful for you to keep a journal and take a few minutes at the beginning and/or the end of the day or week to reflect on what you have done.

What can we do better?

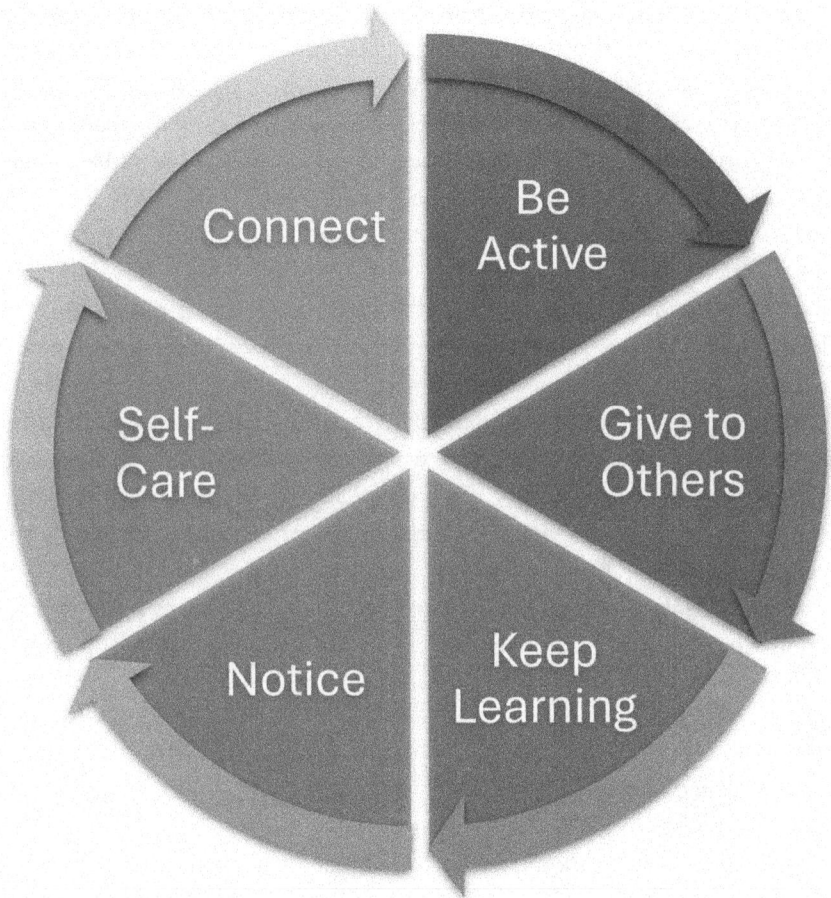

Figure 9.1 Six ways to wellbeing framework

This does bring us on to the topic of time, which always comes up when wellbeing is discussed. "I don't have time" is what I often hear – it is also what I often tell myself! It is important to acknowledge that time is often scarce and time for wellbeing often gets used for seemingly more important things! It is wonderful to find the time for a long walk or run, or to go on a spa day with friends, or to take time reading a book. However, wellbeing does not need to be time-heavy – we can take moments every day.

I speak a lot about micro-moments of wellbeing. This is taking one minute to look out the window, watch the clouds go by, and breathe (notice); it is taking a few minutes to message a family member or friend to say you are thinking about them (connect); it is stopping to really listen to someone, rather than rushing (giving time to others). Find time for the big things, but also make time for those smaller moments that can accumulate across the day and week to fill you (and others) with joy. This is self-care.

The six ways to wellbeing framework has also been used to create a wellbeing curriculum for children and young people (Gillard et al., 2024), which enables this idea of embracing wellbeing all the time. This intervention links the six ways to wellbeing with Acceptance and Commitment Therapy (ACT) approaches to offer lesson plans, activities, and resources to develop thinking, understanding, and engagement with wellbeing on a day-to-day, lifelong way. While designed for children and young people, the messages and activities are equally useful for adults and can promote an ethos of wellbeing that appreciates the individual differences and celebrates wellbeing for all.

Learning is one of the areas of wellbeing, and we know that learning engagement is facilitated by a positive feeling of wellbeing. We will now explore learning in more detail, considering the importance of autonomy and creativity in learning.

Personalisation and choice in learning. Several responses reflected children's desire for more autonomy, authentic choice, and creative approaches to education:

- *"I like to choose what I learn . . . choosing between two worksheets is not real choice."*
- *"School needs to have a more creative approach."*
- *"Subject content should be relative to real-life situations."*

These responses point to a broader need for curriculum reform that allows for personal interests, life skills, and alternative learning styles. These perspectives align with **Self-Determination Theory** (Deci and Ryan, 2000), which asserts that autonomy, competence, and relatedness are essential for intrinsic motivation and psychological wellbeing. Niemiec and Ryan (2009) found that autonomy-supportive environments lead to higher academic engagement and emotional wellbeing.

Small group settings and safe spaces. Children spoke about the benefits of reduced class sizes, safe withdrawal spaces, and calm environments. This was especially important for those with additional needs or anxiety:

- *"Being in a room with fewer pupils."*
- *"Having a free pass to leave class when anxious helps."*
- *"I was allowed to go to learning support . . . but wasn't learning anything."*

This is supported by Florian and Black-Hawkins (2011), who argue that inclusive education must involve **adjusting the environment** rather than expecting the child to conform. A neurodiversity-affirming approach challenges deficit-based models, viewing neurodivergent children not as disordered or deficient, but as having different cognitive profiles that bring unique strengths, perspectives, and needs, which should be understood, respected, and supported within inclusive school environments. Some children identified systemic issues, including rigid timetables, inappropriate curriculum, and punitive discipline systems:

- *"The resources aren't there or the skills to nurture children."*
- *"The school remained rigid in their policies."*
- *"School didn't give proper authentic choices."*

The comments show that children value relationships, trust, respect, and emotional safety above all. Schools that adopt relational, flexible, and inclusive approaches are more likely to meet the needs of these students. There is a clear call for improved consistency in support, attention to mental health, meaningful social connection, and more responsive, individualised learning environments.

The impacts of unconscious bias

The statistics tell us one story, but we also hear testimony from children who feel the effects of living and learning within a system that was, and still is, built on white supremacy. It is within living memory for many Black Caribbean families that their children were routinely placed into special education units, due to concerns they were "educationally subnormal". Researchers as early as the 1970s identified that teachers had lower expectations of their Black Caribbean students compared to their other peers (Coard, 1971), but this phenomenon has persisted into the new millennium, with disparities in the use of suspension; the numbers of children in alternative provision placements or Pupil Referral Units; and overall achievement at key stage 4 and 5. The picture is similarly bleak for children from a Roma-Gypsy background. The Timpson Review of 2019, which looked in detail at exclusions (now referred to as Suspension for fixed terms or Permanent Exclusions for removal completely from a school roll), found that Roma-Gypsy children are three to four times more likely to be excluded than their white British peers (the intersectionality of poverty, school attendance, and SEND are also huge levers here). It calls to mind a colleague's comment, without any malice intended, that they had a really challenging GCSE class, but that it was not that surprising to them when they considered it was "mainly Roma-Gyspy children".

How aware are most staff in schools of their own biases, regardless of their own race, background, or personal views? White staff can feel uncomfortable, even offended, by discussions around race. We see lots of debate online around the exclusion statistics, with commentators eager to poke holes in data and polish off the teacher halo. However, the reality, time and time again, is that some racial groups benefit more from our education system than others; some parents feel more welcomed than others; and we are quick to pre-judge students even based on how their name sounds (Childs and Wooten, 2022).

Most people who work with children, or work in a school in some capacity, will be aware of the Child Q case in 2022 (following the initial incident in December of 2020). For those who don't recognise the case, there were protests in east London following the release of a safeguarding review into a 15-year-old Black girl being strip-searched at her school. The details of the incident were horrific, and the review found that racism was likely to have been a factor in the devastating decisions that the adults made that day, and on the treatment the girl was subjected to. This sparked many discussions about the adultification particularly of Black children, whereby children are seen as and treated as older and more capable than their developmental stage or age would suggest. Research has shown that white respondents in surveys perceive Black girls as needing less protection than their white counterparts and less nurture. They also perceive them as more sexually aware and active (Epstein et al., 2017). How can we expect our Black girls to feel safe, supported, and nurtured in school against a backdrop of systemic and deep-rooted racism?

It is not enough to run a once-a-year anti-racism training session. If UK schools are going to become truly aware of their biases and systemic racial barriers, there needs to be a whole school approach that looks at and confronts racism head on; diversifies staff and leadership; talks with the community and children to engage their voices in decision-making; and reviews policies, curricula, and data. Anti-racism is not celebrating a key event once a year and moving on, and it's not some posters up in the corridor.

Uniform: The silver bullet or prison of the body?

I (Louise) can hand on heart admit that I was once a uniform advocate. I truly believed that it represented a culture of sweating the small stuff. As a newly qualified teacher, more experienced staff would tell me that if you can sweat the small stuff, the big stuff doesn't happen, meaning if I zoomed in on the smallest infringements, then bigger issues would never materialise. Experience, time, and research showed me that simply wasn't the case. Research (albeit in the USA) has shown that at the primary level, schools that insisted on uniform did not have more prosocial behaviour, or better attendance, than schools who had no uniform (Ansari et al., 2022). This is echoed by the many leaders who have been within the MAT system, and also in the world outside of mainstream. Damian Belshaw, for example, Head of InClude alternative provision, shared the following:

> uniform is always a simple (and false) yardstick to measure behaviour. In reality it doesn't matter! I've seen the best schools in the world and they had minimal uniform rules! I know some . . . trusts that go on about them merely because it's something they can "control".

The debate has raged for years and becomes louder around September/October time when we see a flurry of articles in the news from disgruntled parents of children who have fallen foul of a particularly harsh new rule in their school. It appears we need to go beyond the headlines and emotion and look at what the rationale might be for school uniforms:

- **Safeguarding:** it is much easier to identify a stranger on site, or student from another school, if they are not in uniform.
- **Belonging:** uniforms can create a sense of belonging to a community, pride in your school, and identifying something in common with other students.
- **Cost:** for some families having one uniform to buy once a year is easier than having to keep a wardrobe updated.
- **Reduces bullying:** with no labels or fashion statements readily available, it can reduce the impact of feeling isolated and different due to poverty.
- **Compliance:** teaches students that there are certain rules in the outside world that we have to follow to be successful in our lives and careers.

I would argue that each of these reasons is at least misguided, but inherently wrong at worst. Let's start with safeguarding: there is commonsense in the rationale described, but it ignores the impact that suspensions or isolation for incorrect uniforms can have on psychological safety, as well as the risk of vulnerable children not being in their school whilst serving a suspension. Furthermore, there is evidence to suggest that certain groups of children are more policed than others for uniform infractions, especially girls, gender non-conforming children, and neurodiverse children. Whilst the argument for creating a sense of "belonging" can feel intoxicating, especially when we live in a society that can feel so disparate and isolated, children are consistently telling us the opposite. Reidy (2021, p. 7) put this argument to bed so aptly in her research on the impacts of uniform on health and education: "belonging is fostered by a supportive, respectful atmosphere and a sense of achieving".

This feels a hundred miles away from what young people have been telling us. When asked what would make school a better environment, one respondent replied (Popoola and Sivers, 2023: *"Not being told off for loosening my tie and untucking my shirt because it is so uncomfortable"*.

As an adult, if our jacket is too warm, we take it off. If we find our shirt uncomfortable, we don't wear it again. Students often don't have this freedom to even regulate their level of physical comfort without asking permission. Does this say more about the need to control children and their bodies than our desire to make them feel part of a community?

This leads us to the idea of compliance. Yes, the world has rules we all need to follow; there is a social code in every area of life. However, where do we draw the line? When we insist a student wear their hair a particular way (which correlates with racialised ideas of what is "smart" hair and the disproportionate rates of punishment of children with afro hair), we might be trying to remind them that the world around them has certain expectations, but we are also inadvertently impinging on the child's right to freedom of expression (Article 12 of the UN Convention on the Rights of the Child).

Lastly, we know that uniforms can become prohibitively expensive for families of growing children, especially when we consider they can only buy items from specific shops and also have to buy multiple different PE kits, blazers, ties, and all the paraphernalia we have become obsessed with.

Do we throw the baby out with the bath water? I would argue, no. Let's keep the good parts of a uniform policy. Let's design simple, cheap, and comfortable uniforms for our schools, which students may be more willing to wear in the first place: a pair of black jogging bottoms or chinos, a polo shirt in whichever colour, and a sweatshirt with a school logo (if we really feel strongly inclined!). Let's involve students and parents in the design process; after all, they are the ones buying and wearing uniforms, respectively. Perhaps making these brave and counter-culture decisions is truly what we meant by sweating the small stuff.

What next?

Read widely, listen to podcasts, attend seminars, talk to colleagues, and decide what you want to do and how and when you'll do it. We need every person who works in and with schools to be on this mission with us together. The mood is changing; people are questioning the system now more than ever, and we are reaching the climax of the crisis in our education system. The question of what comes after the storm depends on each of us doing our part as an individual and collectively – considering what is achievable for you in your context and within your role. What we want our education system to look and feel like is laid out in this book, and has been advocated for so clearly by the very people we are meant to serve: children.

It is children and young people who are the reason for us writing this book and continuing with the work we have done for many years. We are inspired by their insights, their ideas, and their desire to learn and grow. We need to create an education system that nurtures this growth, right now and for the generations ahead. We need to keep learning, innovating, and collaborating. So, what are we waiting for? Let's transform and dare to reimagine an education system that is fit for all.

References

Aked, J., Marks, N., Cordon, C., and Thompson, S., 2008. Five ways to wellbeing: A report presented to the Foresight Project on communicating the evidence base for improving people's well-being. New Economics Foundation.

Ansari, A., Shepard, M., and Gottfried, M.A., 2022. School uniforms and student behavior: Is there a link? *Early Childhood Research Quarterly*, 58, pp. 278–286.

Armstrong, T., 2010. *Neurodiversity: Discovering the Extraordinary Gifts of Autism, ADHD, Dyslexia, and Other Brain Differences*. Cambridge, MA: Da Capo Press.

Basarkod, G., 2019. The six ways to well-being (6W-WeB): A new measure of valued action that targets the frequency and motivation for six behavioural patterns that promote well-being. Australian Catholic University [online]. Available at: https://www.basarkod.com/sixways.

Bath, H., 2008. The three pillars of trauma-informed care. *Reclaiming Children and Youth*, 17(3), pp. 17–21.

Bergin, C. and Bergin, D., 2009. Attachment in the classroom. *Educational Psychology Review*, 21(2), pp. 141–170.

Blodgett, C. and Lanigan, J.D., 2018. The association between Adverse Childhood Experience (ACE) and school success in elementary school children. *School Psychology Quarterly*, 33(1), pp. 137–146.

Bowlby, J., 1969. *Attachment and Loss, Volume I: Attachment*. London: Hogarth Press.

Childs, T.M. and Wooten, N.R., 2022. Teacher bias matters: An integrative review of correlates, mechanisms, and consequences. *Race Ethnicity and Education*, 26(3), pp. 368–397. https://doi.org/10.1080/13613324.2022.2122425.

Coard, B., 1971. Making black children subnormal in Britain. *Integrated Education: Race and Schools*, 9(5), pp. 49–52.

Deci, E.L. and Ryan, R.M., 2000. The "what" and "why" of goal pursuits: Human needs and the self-determination of behavior. *Psychological Inquiry*, 11(4), pp. 227–268.

Epstein, R., Blake, J.L., and González, T., 2017. Girlhood Interrupted: The Erasure of Black Girls' Childhood [online]. Available at: https://genderjusticeandopportunity.georgetown.edu/wp-content/uploads/2020/06/girlhood-interrupted.pdf [Accessed 3 November 2022].

Florian, L. and Black-Hawkins, K., 2011. Exploring inclusive pedagogy. *British Educational Research Journal*, 37(5), pp. 813–828.

Gillard, D., Grindle, C., Hooper, N., Jackson-Brown, F., and Hancock, R., 2024. *The Science of Children's Wellbeing: Practical Sessions to Support Children Aged 7 to 11*. Abingdon: Routledge.

Maslow, A.H., 1943. A theory of human motivation. *Psychological Review*, 50(4), pp. 370–396.

Niemiec, C.P. and Ryan, R.M., 2009. Autonomy, competence, and relatedness in the classroom. *Theory and Research in Education*, 7(2), pp. 133–144.

Perry, B.D., 2006. *The Boy Who Was Raised as a Dog: And Other Stories from a Child Psychiatrist's Notebook*. New York: Basic Books.

Pianta, R.C., Steinberg, M., and Rollins, K., 2003. The first two years of school: Teacher–child relationships and deflections in children's classroom adjustment. *Development and Psychopathology*, 7(2), pp. 295–312.

Popoola, M. and Sivers, S., 2023. Pupil views research: Children's perspectives on school and mental health. Unpublished internal report.

Reidy, J., 2021. Reviewing school uniform through a public health lens: Evidence about the impacts of school uniform on education and health. *Public Health Review*, 16(42), pp. 1–17.

Skinner, B.F., 1953. *Science and Human Behavior.* New York: Macmillan.

Thorsborne, M. and Blood, P., 2013. *Implementing Restorative Practices in Schools: A Practical Guide to Transforming School Communities.* London: Jessica Kingsley Publishers.

Timpson Review, 2019. Timpson Review of School Exclusion 2019 [online]. Available at: https://assets.publishing.service.gov.uk/government/uploads/system/uploads/attachment_data/file/807862/Timpson_review.pdf.

Recommended further reading/listening

Fritzgerald, A. and Rice, S. (2020). *Antiracism and Universal Design for Learning: Building Expressways to Success.* Lynnfield, MA: CAST Professional Publishing.

Hammond, Z., 2015. *Culturally Responsive Teaching and the Brain: Promoting Authentic Engagement and Rigor Among Culturally and Linguistically Diverse Students.* Thousand Oaks, CA: Corwin.

Shanks, R.K., Ovington, J., Cross, B., and Carnarvon, A.D. (2023). *School Uniforms: New Materialist Perspectives.* Cham: Palgrave Macmillan.

Index

Note: For figure citations, page numbers appear in *italics*. For table citations, page numbers appear in **bold**.

ableism 27
abuse: types of 11, 51
academic pressure 90–107; curriculum inflexibility 119
acceptance 7–8
Acceptance and Commitment Therapy (ACT) 54–5, 162
accountability 8, 25, 82
ACT Matrix 55, *57*, 57–8
active listening 61
adaptability 82
ADHD *see* attention deficit hyperactivity disorder (ADHD)
adolescence 71
adverse childhood experiences (ACEs) 7, 10, 17, 51, 103
after-school clubs 123
AI *see* artificial intelligence (AI)
alternative provision 115–16
analytical thinking 61
anxiety 9, 11, 42, 47, 67, 72, 112, 117, 157–8, 162; separation 112
Applied Behaviour Analysis 29
apprenticeships 96
art 93
artificial intelligence (AI) 91; *see also* ChatGPT
assessment: formative 106; self-assessment 106; summative 106
Atkins, P. 54
attachment theory 51, 157
ATTEND framework 122–4
attendance 33, 101, 109–28, 164; absence rates 110; academic pressure 119; alternative provision 115–16; at-risk ages 112; autonomy and voice 119; barriers to 111–13; bullying 118; child-focused approach 113–22; compassion and kindness 126–7; crisis 122, 127; curriculum inflexibility 119; EOTAS 115–16; home education 116; issues and problems 109–13; local authorities 115–16, 130–7; maintaining factors 111; mental health issues 116; persistent and severe absence 110; physical safety concerns 119–20; precipitating factors 111; predisposing factors 111; reasonable adjustments 122; relationships 121; school environment 118–19; school placements, appropriacy of 114–15; SEND 114, 116, 118; senior leadership team (SLT) 132–3; suspensions 10; trauma 116, 119–20; unsafe environments 118; vulnerable groups 110–11; *see also* ATTEND framework; Mental Health Support Teams (MHST)
attention deficit hyperactivity disorder (ADHD) 114, 118, 120
austerity 17, 143
authoritarian approach 52
authoritativeness 37
autism spectrum conditions 112, 114, 120
autonomy 3, 23, 25–6, 37, 100, 107, 119, 121–2; concept of 100

backchat 38
Barnardo's Scotland 20–1
Beacon House 58
behaviour: approaches 34–7; management 48, 87; point systems 28–31, 42; policies 8–10

Index

behavioural psychology 8
behaviourism 9, 29, 50, 71, 87, 94, 159
belonging 6, 42, 85–7, 111, 121, 166; concept of 8; uniforms 165
Belshaw, D. 165
bereavement 112
bilingualism 97
bioecological model *141*, 150
Black Panther Party 90
Black students 29; Caribbean students 163; girls 164
Black-Hawkins, K. 163
Blodgett, C. 159
Blood, P. 159
'bottom-up' approach 53
brain development 38
break/lunch times 123–4
British Psychological Society (BPS) 32
Bronfenbrenner, U. 141
Brummer, J. 37
Brunzell, T. 37
budgeting skills *see* financial management
bullying 45–7, 56, 70, 111, 118; anti-bullying **57**, 86; uniforms 165
burnout 25, 117

CAMHS (Child and Adolescent Mental Health Services) 71, 73
care 85
Carter, J. 24
change 53; curriculum 100–1
Chapman, S. 34–6
ChatGPT 92; *see also* artificial intelligence (AI)
chemistry 13
chemotherapy 30
child development 10–12
child psychology 10
Child Q case (2022) 164
children missing education (CME) 110–11, 135
Children's Society: Good Childhood Report (2022) 67
Chinese language 97
Chinese students 111
choice in learning 162
chronosystem *141*, 143, 151
Citizens UK 24
Class Dojo 29
cognitive science 11
collaboration 8, 58, 82, 105

Common Assessment Framework (CAF) 36
communication: clarity of 81, 133; consistency of 81; skills 99
community 16; empowerment programmes 90–1; hubs 17; relationships 84–5
Compass 34–7; CAF 36, 42
compass metaphor 59
compassion 21–5, 37, 94, 111, 126–7
competence 3, 23, 100–1, 107; inquiry-based learning 103
compliance 42, 166
computer usage 33
computing 13
conflict: avoidance 38; resolution **55**, 86
connectedness 56, **57**, 92–4, 111
connection 7–8, 17, 26, 42, 64; before correction 127
content: diversity and 90–1; redesigning 90–2
continuous professional development (CPD) 15–16, 23, 62, 77
contributions and benefits **55**
cooperative group dynamics **55**
cooperative learning 86
Core Design Principles (CDPs) 54–8, **55**
core work skills 60–1
cost-of-living crisis 143
Covid-19 pandemic 3–4, 122, 138–54; 2-metre rule 139; case studies 142; catch-up learning 144–5, 148–9; chronosystem 143, 151; community system 144–5; crisis 148–50; exosystem 145, 152; family system 143–5; homeschool 93; impact of 7, 146–50, 154; influence and impact, systemic layers of 140–6; language development, impact on 150; lockdown and 3, 35, 45–7, 139, 143; lost learning 145, 148; macrosystem 145–6, 151–2; media coverage 145; memories of 140; Mental Health Support Teams (MHST) 73; mesosystem 144, 152–3; microsystems 143–4, 153; peer group systems 144; safety 146–8; school system 144–5; teaching, perceptions of 14; travel restrictions 143
creative thinking 61
creativity 16
culturally responsive practices 86
culture 112

171

Index

Culture of Error 31
curiosity *see* interest/curiosity
curriculum change 99–106
Curriculum Review (2025) 149–50
customer service 61

Deci, E. L. 23, 32, 37
decision-making: fair and inclusive **55**
deficit-based models 163
depression 11, 67
Designated Safeguarding Leads (DSLs) 17, 19–20, 36
DfE (Department for Education) 13–14, 18, 49, 73–4, 88, 133, 135; *Working Together to Improve School Attendance* guidance 124–5, 130–1
difference 7–9, 34, 42, 145–6, 163
disconnectedness 107
discrimination 51
disengagement 42, 107, 136
distressing experiences 159
diverse representation: curriculum 86
Dix, P. 87, 94
dyslexia 119
dysregulation 32, 38

early years education 1–2
Edu-Twitter 11
Education Act: Section 19 pathway 124–5, 134
Education Health and Care Plans (EHCPs) 115, 118, 120
Education Mental Health Practitioners (EMHP) 73
Education Welfare Service 131–2
Educational Psychologists 4, 6, 21, 62–3, 73, 138
EHCNA (education, health, and care needs assessments) 6–7
elective home education (EHE) 135–7
emotion: awareness 39; boundary-setting 39; coaching 39–40, 42; emotional support 85; empathy 39; naming 39; problem-solving 39; understanding 39; validation 39
emotional distress 117
emotional exhaustion 25
emotional literacy 60, 112
Emotional Literacy Support Assistant (ELSA) 32, 78, 123
emotional needs 158
emotional psychology 11
emotional regulation 112, 114

emotional resilience 41
emotional safety 26, 42, 121–2
emotional wellbeing 20, 69
Emotionally Based School Avoidance (EBSA) 110
empathy 8, 61, 102
engagement 104
English: language 97; as a subject 101
enrichment 93
entrepreneurial challenges 105
environmental adjustment 163
EOTAS (Education Other Than at School) 115–16, 120, 128
ethnicity 10, 112, 163–4
ethos and environment 74–6, 111
exams 70, 111; *see also* assessment; GCSEs (General Certificate of Secondary Education); SAT results
exclusion 72; *see also* suspensions
exosystem *141*, 145, 152
exploration 104–5
extracurricular engagement 86

fairness 16, 82
family 46; dynamics, changes in 112; stress 112; system 143–4
fear 70; of punishment 117
fear-and-shame-based systems 37
feedback 15
Felitti, V. J. 51
fight-flight response 38, 40
financial decision-making activity 105
financial management 104–7
Finland 107; education system 95–7
'fitting in' 8
Fixed Term Exclusion 32, 34
'flattening the grass' approaches 28–33
flexibility 61, 121
Florian, L. 163
fMRI scans 10
follow-through, lack of 158
food technology 93
Ford Motor Company 24
formative assessment *see* assessment
free school meals 110
freedom of expression 166
friendships 37, 46–7, 111, 121, 158

GCSEs (General Certificate of Secondary Education) 70, 72, 83, 93, 95–6, 101, 164
'Get into teaching' adverts 14

Index

Gillard, D. 54–5
Google 92
Gottman, J. 39
group collaboration 105
growth mindset 82
Gundlach, H. 14
Gypsy/Roma community 111, 163–4

Harris, W. 134
headteachers 18, 25, 28
helpful/unhelpful actions **55**
Hierarchy of Needs 148
history lessons 91–2
Holding, M. 91
home education 113, 116; effective 135–6; *see also* elective home education (EHE)
homework 70
homophobia 27, 51
Hougaard, R. 24
HPA (hypothalamic–pituitary–adrenal) 11
humanity 7–8

identity: identity-affirming practices 86; shared group **55**
in-service education and training (INSET) 134
InClude alternative provision 165
inclusion 5–6, 82; concept of 6; definition of 5–6; inclusive social norms 86
inconsistency 158
individualism 3
information: analysis 105; organisation 105
Initial Child Protection Conference (ICPCs) 20
innovation 82
inquiry-based learning 98, 101–5, 107
INSET (in-service education and training) 36
interest/curiosity 56, **57**, 61, 85
International Baccalaureate (IB) 97–9, 107; learners 98; learning community 99; teaching 98–9
international schools 97
intrinsic motivation 30–1, 42, 162
isolation rooms/booths 28, 32–3, 42, 119

Jones, R. 50
journey to school 111

Kim, J. 14
kindness 6, 37, 63–4, 86, 94, 111, 121, 126–7, 136; redesigning 90–2
Kohn, A. 30–2

Labour government (UK) 32, 100
Lanigan, J. D. 159
Latimer, L. H. 90
leadership 26, 61, 75; principles *81*; shared 82
learning skills: approaches to 99; concept of 60
learning theories 11
Lemov, D. 31
Lewis, J. 28
life lessons 93
life-long learning 61, 107, 152
local authorities (LAs) 115–16, 125, 130–7; delays and provision, lack of 115–16
lockdown *see* Covid-19 pandemic
logos 15
Looney, E. 4

macrosystem *141*, 145–6, 151–2
mainstream schools 157; resourcing, lack of 7
Mandela, N. 27
Mannion, J. 99
marking policies 15–16
masking 117
Maslow, A. H. 148; Hierarchy of Needs 158–9
mathematics 13, 101
Maxwell Martin, A. 126
melatonin 97
menstruation 100, 119
mental health 5, 13–26; change and 79; chronic conditions 68; core principles 74; curriculum teaching and learning 76; disorder, definition of 68; emotional distress and 117; emotional needs 158; ethos and environment 75–6; external referrals 78–9; government initiatives 72–4; history of difficulties 112; home education 135–7; identifying need 78; issues and problems 67–72; mentally healthy schools 67–88; monitoring support 78; parent and carer involvement 79; parental 84, 112; relationships 80–5; school attendance 116; school solutions 72–4; staff

173

Index

development 77–8; statistics 67–9, 87; student voice 77; support systems 75; targeted support 78–9; WHO definition 67
Mental Health Support Improving Attendance Team (MIAT) 125–6, 128
Mental Health Support Teams (MHST) 78, 88, 125; functions of 73–4; s 19 legislation 124–6
mentoring programmes 86
mesosystem *141*, 144, 152–3
metacognitive skills 60
microsystems *141*, 143–4, 153
model students 38
monitoring: agreed actions **55**
motivation 61, 91, 101; psychology of 100, 106; see also intrinsic motivation
multi-academy trusts (MATs) 23, 28, 32, 130, 165
multimedia presentations 99
mutual respect 82

NASUWT (teaching union) 15
National Institute for Health and Care Excellence (NICE): Social, Emotional, and Mental Health in Primary and Secondary Schools guidelines 5, 49
National Society for Prevention of Cruelty to Children (NSPCC) 21
neglect 147
neonatal care 7
neuroscience 10–12, 28, 39–40, 42
Newton, H. 90
NHS (National Health Service) 145
'no child left behind' 7
Nottingham City Educational Psychology Service 4

ODD (Oppositional Defiant Disorder) 114
Ofsted inspections 71, 96, 142
Ogunlade, C. 36–7
open lessons 16
oracy skills 99, 102
Ostrom, E. 54
'out of school' 113–14

Paglayan, A. S. 28–9
pandemic see Covid-19 pandemic
panic attacks 47, 117
parenting styles 39
participation 86

pastoral teams 17
Payne Bryson, T. 34
performance-orientated classrooms 111
Perry, B. 51, 59
persistent absenteeism (PA) 110–11
personal action plans 106
personalisation 162
phonics 71
physical education (PE) 93
physics 13
Piaget, J. 10
Pianta, R. C. 157–8
podcasts 167
police brutality 90
Popoola, M. 4, 30, 37, 134
postgraduate certificate in education (PGCE) 10, 13
poverty 164
power asymmetry 83
pressure 3; academic 90–107; exams and homeworks 70
Primary Years Program (PYP) 97–8
principals see headteachers
process-person-context-time (PPCT) model 140
professional development 23; see also continuous professional development (CPD)
professionalism 16, 24
Progress 8 scores 71
prosocial approaches 54–6, 58, 64; behaviour 165; concept of 54; relational ethos 56
provocation 104
psychological partners 80, 125, 157
psychological safety 69, 166
psychological theory 12
psychology: education and 8–9; outdated 94
puberty 97
public speaking 102–3
punishment, fear of 117
punitive approaches 28–33; behaviour systems 10, 159
Pupil Referral Units 163
pupil views 68; journey 3–5
Pupil Views Collaborative Group 4–5
PYP IB Inquiry Cycle 104

race 29, 163–4
racism 27, 51, 90–1, 164; anti-racism training 164
reasonable adjustments 122

Index

recommendations 156–67
'red or green' update system 8–9
reductionism 9
regulation 42; *see also* dysregulation; self-regulation
relatedness 23–4, 37, 69, 100, 107; concept of 101; inquiry-based learning 103
relational approaches 48–50, 64; definition of 48–50
relational consistency 122
relational curriculum 60–1
relational ethos 53–4; prosocial approach 56; trauma-informed approach 58–60
relational learning environment 60; inclusive 62
relational power: of supervision 62–3
relational practices 42
relational trauma 50–3
relationships 45–64, 126; children's views 46; community and school 84–5; dynamic 47–8; importance of 45, 157; mental health 80–5; peer or staff 111; poor 3, 70; positive 86, 121; shifting 47–8; SLT and organisation 80–2; staff and students 82–6
research 104–5; skills 99
resilience 60–1
respect 16, 157, 121–2; for teaching 13–14
restlessness 38
restorative approaches 29, 35; practices 86, 159
Review Panel report (March 2025) 100
riots 143
ritual humiliation 28
Robinson, K. 24–5
Rogers, C. 40
rounds, concept of 24
rules 10, 27–42, 70; *see also* behaviour approaches; emotion; punitive approaches; trauma-informed approaches; uniforms
Ryan, R. M. 23, 32, 37

safe spaces 162
safeguarding 17, 33, 118, 164, 166
safety 87; concerns 119–20; concept of 146; Covid-19 pandemic 146–8; emotional 26, 42, 121–2; as a human right 52; psychological 69, 166
sanction system 72

SAT results 71
school: attendance *see* attendance; audits 74–9; climate or culture 111; Covid-19, impact of *see* Covid-19 pandemic; current systems, critique of 9–10; education and 1–3; environment 118–19; mainstream *see* mainstream schools; phase 111; placements, appropriacy of 114–15; rules *see* rules; size 111; whole school approach 134
school-centred initial teacher training (SCITT) 13
science subjects 101
Seale, B. 33, 90
secondary school, transition to 111
self-assessment *see* assessment
self-awareness 8, 61
self-determination theory (SDT) 23, 32, 100, 102, 107, 162
self-esteem 41, 97, 102
self-harm 71
self-management skills 99
self-organisation 104
self-reflection 32
self-regulation 41
seminars 167
SEN Code of Practice 149
SEND *see* special educational needs and disabilities (SEND)
senior leadership team (SLT) 15, 17–18, 23, 70–2, 77, 80–2, 132–3
Senior Mental Health Lead (SMHL) 18–19, 25, 73, 78
sensory environment 111
sensory overload 119
sensory processing 114
service orientation 61
severely persistent absenteeism (SPA) 110
sexism 27
sexual assault 119
sexual awareness 164
Shakespeare, W. 152
shame 42
Shark Tank 105
showcases 105
Siegel, D. 34
silence 10, 38
Sivers, S. 4, 30, 37, 99
Skinner, B. F. 29
sleep 97, 113
small group settings 162

175

Index

social conditioning 87
Social Emotional Aspects of Learning (SEAL) 35, 39
social influence 61
social media 67, 69
social networks 86
social skills 96, 99, 139; Covid-19 pandemic, impact of 149
socialisation 8
socio-economic attainment gap 150
'sorting out' 105
special educational needs and disabilities (SEND) 29, 76, 114, 116, 118, 164; crisis 2; school attendance 110, 112, 120, 128, 130, 132–3, 136; teacher demands 14–15
special educational needs co-ordinators (SENCOs) 19, 118
Square Pegs 122
staff: development 77–8; relationships 82–4; supervision 19–21; wellbeing 13–26; *see also* training
stress 3, 11, 70, 112, 158
strip searches 164
structure of school day 111
student voice 77, 86
summative assessment *see* assessment
supervision 26; key staff 19–21; relational power of 62–3
supportive school climate 86
surveillance 28, 33
survival: instincts 8; skills 93
suspensions: ethnicity and 10; isolation booths 32–3

talent management 61
Tavistock and Portman NHS Trust 21
teacher-twitter 11
Teachers on Screen Project 14
teachers 47; holidays and working hours 14; shortages 13; unpaid work 15; workload 14–15
teaching and learning responsibilities (TLR) 17
teamwork 102
technology: Covid-19 pandemic 143, 150–2; impact on childhood 127; literacy 61
thinking skills 99
Thorsborne, M. 159
Times Education Supplement (TES) 28
Timpson Review (2019) 163–4

Tobias, A. 122, 128
toilet breaks 33, 100, 118
token economies 31
'top-down' approach 53
training 62; *see also* continuous professional development (CPD); staff
transparency 81
trauma: developmental 37; impact of 10–12; relational 50–3; school attendance 119–20; traumatic events 112
trauma-informed approaches 35, 37–9, 42, 54, 118, 159; relational ethos 58–60; school attendance 116
Traveller of Irish Heritage 111
Treisman, K. 50–1, 59
trust 16, 56, **57**, 81
'trusted adults' 126

unconditional positive regard 40–2, 127
unconscious bias 163–4
uniforms 30, 123, 133, 165–7; belonging 165; bullying and 165; compliance 165; cost 165; incorrect 32; parental input 167; rules 42; safeguarding 165; shoes 10; suggestions for change 166–7
United Nations (UN): happiness index 95–6
United Nations Convention on the Rights of the Child (UNCRC); Article 12 166
United States (US): Black communities 90–1; community empowerment programmes 90–1; uniforms 165
University College London (UCU) 21
unsafe environments 118, 159

violence 11, 118, 147
vocational pathways 96
voice 16; *see also* student voice 119
Vygotsky, L. 10

Wales: new curriculum 94–5
'warm strict' approach 28
Waters, S. 16–17
weapons 118
webinars 4
welcoming environments 86
wellbeing 42; culture of 18, 39; emotional 20, 162; eudaimonic 159; framework 160, *161*; hedonic 160;

hubs 63; learning and 162; micro-moments of 161–2; performative 25; promotion of 159–63; psychological 37; scores 15; 'six ways to wellbeing' framework *161*; staff 13–26; support and 82; time for 161
Wellbeing Survey Report (2023/2024) 15
'whole school' approach 88, 134
Wonde attendance recording system 131
World Economic Forum (WEF) 61

World Health Organization (WHO) 11; mental health, definition of 67
World War II 92
worry 70; *see also* anxiety

Yeats, W. B. 31
young carers 112

zero tolerance 9–10, 29, 49, 144, 146, 152
Zuniga-Montanez, R. 150

For Product Safety Concerns and Information please contact our EU
representative GPSR@taylorandfrancis.com
Taylor & Francis Verlag GmbH, Kaufingerstraße 24, 80331 München, Germany

www.ingramcontent.com/pod-product-compliance
Lightning Source LLC
Chambersburg PA
CBHW071742150426
43191CB00010B/1657